The Daley Record

MY FOOTBALL LIFE

TONY DALEY

First Edition.
First published 2022

Published by:
Morgan Lawrence Publishing Services Limited
Ridge House Annexe
16 Main Ridge West
Boston
Lincolnshire
PE21 6QQ
www.morganlawrence.co.uk
email: info@morganlawrence.co.uk
Company number: 12910264

ISBN: 9781838232979

A CIP catalogue record is available for this book from the British Library.

Photographs are courtesy of: PA Images/Alamy Stock, REUTERS/Alamy Stock Photo, David Edsam/Alamy Stock, David Bagnall, All Star Picture Library, Trinity Mirror, Mirrorpix, Action Images/Alex Morton, Adam Fradgley, Michael Regan, Aston Villa Football Club, Wolverhampton Wanderers Football Club.

Every effort has been made to trace the copyright. Any oversight will be rectified in future editions at the earliest opportunity by the publisher.

Edited by David Shuttle
Proofreading by Lois Hide
Cover design by LC Graphix

Printed and bound in Bulgaria
by Pulsio Print.

Dedication

In memory of my parents, Hezekiah and Pernell, who gave me the strength and inspiration to never stop trying.

To my children, Kieran and Sheridan, for whom I will always continue to inspire.

With Love.

Also, by the Author

The Gerry Hitchens Story – From Mine to Milan (2009)
The Bobby Thomson Story – The Real Bobby Dazzler (2010)
Memories Made in Aston (2011)
The Harry Moseley Story – Making It Happen (2012)
La Storia di Gerry Hitchens (Italian version 2014)
Peter Withe – All For The Love of The Game (2017)
Cherno Samba – Still In The Game (2018)
Brian Little – A Little Is Enough (2018)
Jack Grealish – Britain's First £100m Footballer (2021)
An A to Z of Aston Villa (2021)

Acknowledgements

I would like to thank Simon Goodyear, my biographer, who has listened to all of my stories and put them into words to form this book.

Thanks also go to the team at Morgan Lawrence for publishing the book: Mathew Mann, Barrie Pierpoint, Lee Clark, Lois Hide, Peter Taylor and Harry Worgan.

Thank you to David Oliver (Alliance Commercial Finance Limited), and Nigel Waldron (Power Minerals Limited) for sponsoring the book and making it happen.

Lastly, I would like to thank all of the ex-players and managers who have contributed to the Testimonial section with their memories of me as a person and a player.

Tony Daley, 2022.

Contents

FOREWORD BY
Ron Atkinson
Former Aston Villa manager, 1991 - 1994

I HAVEN'T come across too many players like TD. The thing about him was that he was so 'perfect' that I can't remember one issue where he was out of line at all. Now, if you ask me about someone like Dalian (Atkinson), I could tell you a million stories about him. It may sound boring, but TD is what you call a 'perfect professional'. He was easy to work with, Tony trained properly, always got on with it, was never late and was flexible enough that he could play on either wing if we changed things tactically and he never complained about that. He is genuinely a nice fella, a good guy and a pleasure to work with.

TD was probably the fittest player in the club and we didn't half have some pace in that team. Earl Barrett and Dalian were quick, and I'm talking about top-class quick - rapid. The one thing I can remember though was that he made me run faster than I'd ever done before. We (Villa) were playing Arsenal in my second home game and TD picked the ball up on the left-wing and he was facing Lee Dixon at right-back and Tony had him on toast. I was running alongside on the touchline, thinking, "I wish he'd bloody slow down a bit I'm knackered." He really had a good game that day because he really went at Dixon and I think he scored as well. In fact, I think Arsenal were a lucky team for him as I remember him scoring at Highbury for us the following season.

He was an England international and was unlucky not to get more England caps in my mind. I remember commentating on a game that he played in, the one we lost to Sweden in the Euro's.

His dress sense could be called 'outrageous', which was OK – it was stylish, let's say. He always had the best of gear, but at the same time he was always immaculate, and as I say, to an old fogey like me, he was a bit outrageous.

I can't recall ever having any problems with TD; it's hard to remember anything that happened with him. With other players, you can say, "Do you remember (so and so) when he…" Maybe when he was out with the lads he was different but nothing detrimental ever got back to me. However, we played Swindon in the cup away on a Sunday afternoon and we beat them 2 – 1; we were a bit lucky actually. I think Froggy (Steve Froggatt) got a great goal – a pearler. TD played and wasn't playing particularly well. Before the end of the game I said to Andy Gray, my assistant at the time, "Now we've won, have a little pop at TD because their full-back kept bombing on and Tony couldn't stick with him." I went out of the dressing room to listen to the draw for the next round (we drew Liverpool away). When I walked back into the dressing room, Andy was giving Tony dog's abuse – he was laying into him and TD looked quite shaken up. I said to Andy, "Hey Andy, hang on a bit, the lad was having a go, you can't expect him to track back all the time." In the end, Andy cooled it down a bit. Andy then said to me, "You told me to give him a rocket," to which, I replied, "I didn't mean to break him in two! All I meant was to give him a little rocket because we won the game. If we had lost the game I wouldn't have said anything." I found that after winning games was the time to remind people what they didn't do. Andy on that occasion went over the top.

I particularly remember TD playing well in the 'big games', against teams like Liverpool, United and Arsenal. Obviously, he played a major part in the League Cup Final against United at Wembley (March 1994). On the day, I switched Dalian (Atkinson) to the right-wing and TD on the left, so we had a couple of flying machines. I said to them, "If you two don't want to be chasing Parker and Irwin towards our goal, make sure they are running back to their own goal." I told them to "keep running and running" and "if you're absolutely shattered, still keep running, and we'll replace you, but I don't know who with."

Towards the end of his Villa career, we had Froggy coming through and players like David Farrell. I remember getting a phone call when I was out in the States for the World Cup (1994). Graham Taylor (then Wolves manager) wanted to buy TD and had obviously spoken to him and I told Graham that I wouldn't stand in his way if he wanted to join Wolves; I didn't have a problem if he stayed with Villa either. I think part of the problem was that we had a few left-sided players but I left it up to Tony if he wanted to stay or go.

In the end, I think Froggy went to Wolves as well. I thought that was handy – I didn't see that happening.

Ron Atkinson, 2022.

FOREWORD BY
Steve Bull
Former Wolverhampton Wanderers striker, 1986 - 1999

WHEN TONY first came to the Wolves from Villa, he came with Froggy (Steve Froggatt) and they were joined at the hip; they seemed to do everything together at first – they were inseparable and thick as thieves. Me and Thommo (Andy Thompson) were the same when we came from the Albion. We had loads of local lads in our squad at the time, from the Black Country and all of a sudden we got two strange lads from the Villa.

When I first knew Dales and Froggy were coming to the Wolves, they came in high spirits and I thought we'd made two great signings here – absolutely unbelievable. Their club was one of the best clubs in the country at the time but we were stuck in the second tier, having got ourselves up from the Fourth Division. To have them come to our club, it was like having two rough diamonds – absolutely brilliant.

When they first came to Wolves, we all made them welcome and they soon became an important part of the club. However, they soon started being cheeky and came down to our level. There was a lot of rival Villa and Wolves banter. We all thought they came from a big, top club – we thought they were posh and snobby, but it wasn't like that after all.

It took both of them a while to integrate, but once they had learned our 'lingo' and how we worked, they soon got into our mode. The fans didn't take to them straight away, coming from Villa, but as soon as they saw how well they both fitted in or scored a goal, the fans were on side. It was the same for me and Thommo, coming from West Brom – we never looked back.

Every time Thommo was on the physio's couch, I heard a scream and I could hear Thommo shouting, "Bully, Bully." I ran into the physio room and I saw Dales run out the other way. I wondered what was going on and Thommo said, "They're squeezing my leg, Bully, them from Villa, the Villa fans, Bully."

I had to go and grab Dales back and get them to say "sorry" to Thommo. It was like a running joke. It wasn't malicious or anything, it was a joke and a bit of banter.

Talking about the injury table, Dales spent a lot of time on the physio's couch, so much so that we had to get a pair of tweezers because he got so many splinters in his arse from his time sitting on the bench that it wasn't funny!

When Dales was fit and playing alongside Froggy (which didn't happen that much) the two were scary and made my job as a striker really easy. I didn't have to chase back and they provided the balls into the box for me on a plate. On his day, Dales was small, quick, agile and he could cross a good ball – he was unbelievable. It was a shame he didn't play much in the four years he spent at Molineux as he was injury prone, but even so, he became one of the lads in the changing room, nevertheless.

There was only one side of Dales that we couldn't understand and that was his dress sense. He was unbelievable – absolutely scandalous. Dales used to wear the most outrageous clothes that I've ever seen in my life. The colours he used to wear and he had different styled hair. With his gear, we couldn't be bothered to laugh at him but he was the only person in the club who could get away with his clothes. I remember Dales once wore a gold, string vest and gold trousers – he looked like someone out of Pans People, it was scandalous. When we all saw that outfit, he never flinched once, even though we all took the p*** out of him something rotten. He just stood there, looked at us and got on with it. Brilliant!

When Tony came back, I was still at the club in some respect, and it was ironic he came back as a fitness coach as he had spent so much time on the physio's couch – it became our laughing joke within the club. Tony was serious about his fitness role and he loved it – and the lads loved him. They loved his personality and the players took on board exactly what he told them. He was by far the fittest person I've ever known, apart from probably big Cyrille Regis. Dales was always on the weights, but never put weight on – he was just pure muscle, never bulky and he portrayed that both as a player and a fitness coach and still is to this day - he's the same bloke as he's always been.

Steve Bull, 2022.

PROLOGUE BY
Simon Goodyear

I HAVE BEEN lucky enough to work with some of the nicest people in football over the years, including Peter Withe, Brian Little and now Tony Daley. Not only that, but they also have one thing in common – they were three of the most popular Villa players of their respective generations. They were also three of my favourite Villa players too.

Tony joined his hometown club, Aston Villa, as an apprentice at the age of 14 and made his senior debut, aged 17, on 20 April 1985 in a 2–0 defeat at Southampton. He played for Villa for ten seasons, nine at the highest level, and finished a runner-up in both the league seasons of 1989 - 1990 and 1992 - 1993.

He also played in their victorious 1994 League Cup Final against Manchester United at Wembley and nearly got onto the scoresheet, but his shot hit the post and was rebounded by Dalian Atkinson, only for Andrei Kanchelskis to block it with a handball for which he was sent off. Dean Saunders converted the penalty and put Villa 3 – 1 ahead, a score-line which formed the final result and gave Villa a fourth League Cup win. Tony collected what would be the only major trophy of his career.

During this period, Tony was capped seven times for England between 1991 and 1992 under former club manager Graham Taylor. He made his full debut as a substitute in a vital 1 – 1 draw in Poland on 13 November 1991 that saw England qualify for 1992 European Championships. He was subsequently chosen for the squad at the tournament and played in two of England's three games there, but after the tournament he never played for England again.

Tony linked up with Graham Taylor again as he finally left Villa for Wolverhampton Wanderers in July 1994 for a (then) club record £1.25 million, along with his former-Villa teammate, Steve Froggatt, but he was plagued with injuries and was only able to manage 21 appearances for the club in four seasons.

He was signed for the third time in July 1998 by Graham Taylor, who was then Watford manager, on a free transfer. His injury woes continued though and he struggled to get fit, missing most of the final months as the club won promotion to the Premier League. He was given a free transfer to newly promoted Division One side, Walsall in June 1999, and after a six-month spell there, he finished his playing career with Conference side Forest Green Rovers, finally hanging up his boots in July 2002.

As a Villa fan growing up, I watched Tony from the Holte End; it could be said that his immense talent, lightning speed and skill wasn't truly fulfilled in terms of England caps and trophies, let alone appearances. Injury blighted his career, which was a real shame because in the early 1990s, Tony was 'the new kid on the block' and was the one for the present and the future.

Fortunately, Tony also had his head screwed firmly onto his broad shoulders and took a bachelor's degree between 2000 and 2003 whilst playing football part-time and a master's degree between 2008 and 2010. His destiny was to be in Sports Science and fitness and he is now the founder and director of his own company, specialising in fat reduction and muscle gain, bespoke training plans and bespoke nutrition plans. The company is called **7Daley Ltd.**

Simon Goodyear, 2022.
www.goodyearpublications.com

CHAPTER 1
Sweet Dreams Are Made of These

"As a kid, I had a dream of playing for Aston Villa and England."

TO BE PERFECTLY honest, I don't remember too much about my childhood and my introduction to football, so I had to be prompted by my older brother, David, for the purposes of this chapter in my life. My memory isn't what it used to be - I guess it's called getting old! However, once David started talking about that period in my life, I soon recalled those years with happiness. I must also admit, though, that I also dreaded what David was going to say, but thanks to him, we have some words to put down in this section.

I was the youngest of no fewer than seven children (three brothers and three sisters) and we lived with our mum and dad in the Newtown area of Birmingham, which wasn't the best environment it has to be said; we could have gone one of two ways, the wrong way or the right way. However, with the parents we had, we were only heading the right way and were never going to get into trouble. We were brought up properly and taught how to behave and respect others, something that I have taken through to my adulthood.

Mum and Dad were from Jamaica and both came to the UK with the Windrush generation. Dad, called Hezekiah, was born in Westmoreland and came to the UK in 1960, leaving Mum and their four children for 18 months to find a better life and a job, until he was joined by Mum, named Pernell, in 1961. Both Mum and Dad found good jobs together at the Lucas factory in

Birmingham, where they were happy for many years. Four years later, Sandra, Euton, Cobourn and Hyacinth came to join them in Birmingham. During that time, David and Marcia were born in the UK, followed by myself in 1967, completing the family unit.

Mum and Dad worked tirelessly in order to keep us fed and made sure we had a nice home – we never wanted for anything. Looking back, it was tough for them, especially when neither of them really liked football (Dad was more into cricket than anything else). Neither of them had a car but they made sure we got where we wanted to get by bus or lifts from other people. It was hard getting around back then, much harder than it is today but we managed.

David and I attended William Cowper Primary School in Newtown, Birmingham, a stone's throw away from Villa Park, where, unbeknown to me, and a few years' later, I'd be donning the famous claret and blue shirt and playing in front of 40,000 mad Villa fans.

However, that was a few sweet dreams away.

The family home was directly opposite our school, with a stretch of grass and a wall becoming hallowed turf for us. We would pop through the open gate or climb over it when we wanted to play football there. It was standard that I'd be put in goal by my brothers, David & Euton, probably because I was the youngest, but I would come out and run rings around them before repeatedly being hacked down by one of them. It was a great grounding for me, though. My brothers didn't want to hurt me or anything – they just wanted to keep me grounded and it certainly prepared me for what was to come later in my career. I would just react by giggling and taking it as a compliment, just as I did when getting kicked throughout my career, I just got used to it.

Like so many kids I just loved football and would always have a ball with me. Even in the house, my mum would be telling me off because she thought I was going to break stuff! At school we used to play something called 'slams' and, according to David, I hated to lose at it, even though it was only a playground game. 'Slams' was a game where one person would kick the ball against the wall. It would bounce off the wall to the other person, he would side-foot it back and it would carry on like that. Another game we'd play was 'Germans', where you could only score on the volley. There was a park near where we lived where we'd side foot the ball through some iron bars to simulate 'nutmegging', but David seemed to think I cried a lot every time he got the ball off me. Not sure about that bro!

We both always wanted to play football as kids. Even though David is four years older than me, I still wanted to play football with him; I always had a football at my feet, even at the age of eight or nine. I hated being inside the house so it was natural for me (us) to want to go outside, to the park and play football or cricket, or any other ball game. When it rained, we'd play board games like Test Match, Subbuteo or Striker or utilise the plastic fruit Mum had on display in a bowl which we kicked around the house, to the annoyance of our mum. Even on the way to school, we'd be seen kicking a tennis ball to each other – I just wanted to play football all the time. Talking about Subbuteo, I think I've still got all my teams and even the pitch and floodlights.

We both played in the school football team for our respective age groups and even when David left school to join the Navy, I carried on. However, there was a short time near the end of David's time at senior school, that he started to play cricket, but, although I enjoyed playing cricket it was always going to be football for me, so I went off with my other mates to play football.

My brother David was a decent footballer himself and he played for Villa Boys; he thought he was good, but the more I trained and started to run faster, he saw my raw talent develop and I probably overtook him in terms of skill and pace. At William Cowper, I was always the 'star player', and I was the one who stood out from the rest. David remembers one particular game when I took the ball from the kick-off, ran with it down the line and scored without anyone from the opposition touching it. I think it was that game that made people stand up and take notice of Tony Daley.

I always knew that I wanted to play football from an early age, but my education suffered as a result. Even then that was important to me. However, one year I got an average school report – not bad, just average – and my mum came home, didn't say a word and just produced a letter for me to take in the next day. It was a letter saying I wasn't allowed to play any competitive football for three months and that I needed to show improvement with my education. To someone who just wanted to play football all day long, that was a real lesson, a harsh lesson, but one which

I soon understood and turned into a positive later in life. It taught me the importance of education and the importance of being disciplined, doing things right, and I translated that into my playing career and into life after that as well.

The one good thing about my upbringing was that Mum and Dad never stopped either of us playing football. Only after we'd done our homework, of course. Although my parents were very disciplined, they didn't hold any restrictions on me, except where my homework was concerned. I didn't have any complaints about that, as I was always doing something sporty in my spare time, and for me, that was the most important thing in my life.

Having said that, I always loved school (and not just for the sport); I actually enjoyed doing exams and I really wanted to do well; I had no choice really, given that education was something my family was big on – you go to school to learn. So, all-in-all, it was a great time of my life.

I will always remember my introduction to 'hard', competitive football at St. George's School (now St. George's Academy) in Newton, in the playground during breaktimes – it was always the best time of the day for me, especially the hour-long dinner breaks, where we'd organise big games, proper games on grass; we'd often play six against six or 10 against 10. We would put our trainers on and start playing for the rest of the dinner time – it was a big thing at school. It didn't matter about age; you could be a first-year student playing against kids two or three years above you, or more. It was just great to be accepted at that young age and that was a massive thing for me.

One thing I learned from Colin Rogers, my PE teacher at St. George's, was how to use my 'wrong' foot - my left foot. During PE lessons, he told me only to use my left foot during certain sessions; I wasn't allowed to use my right foot at all. That discipline helped my game so much in the future and allowed me to comfortably use both feet.

Sometimes I wouldn't see David for weeks on end and when he'd return from the Navy on leave, he'd notice how much my game had progressed; he'd notice that I would ping balls with both feet across the football field and it was then he knew I was going to be good enough to be a professional footballer. He must have noticed I'd been training to use my left foot because he would see the improvement in me. For me, I always knew in the back of my mind I would play for my favourite club, Aston Villa, at some stage in my life, and I also knew I'd eventually play for England – in fact I dreamt about it. Funnily enough, I seem to recall a schoolteacher ask me one day, "what do you want to do when you leave school?" and when I responded, "I want to be a professional footballer, sir", he said something like, "yeah, yeah, but you have to have a career behind you just in case it doesn't work out." Although I understood what he was saying, I wasn't that interested in doing anything else so I didn't bother too much about finding an alternative career. It wasn't arrogance, I just knew I'd make it as a professional because it was my untold desire to become a footballer that drove me on. I knew I had the talent; David knew I had the talent, so it was up to me to prove to others I had what it took to become a top professional footballer.

The rest is history, as they say.

In the late 1970s and early 1980s when I was still at school, there was a wealth of natural talent around the Birmingham area, and I am certain, most of the lads who didn't make it as a semi-professional or professional footballer would walk into today's professional academies – they were that good; the standard was so high back then, much higher than it is now. If you look at the 12 or 13-year-old lads today, they are all coached to play and you can see most don't have a lot of natural 'flair' and aren't allowed to express themselves anymore – that's such a shame. Of course, there are the exceptions, but in general, football today is about coaching kids to do certain jobs on the football pitch and not to improve natural ability or teach them the basics.

Compared to the young players of my era, and I'm including myself here, I'd say I was a 'flair' player - and I was encouraged to be one as well. It was only the fact that I had something 'special' that I was picked out from the crowd; I could do things that maybe the other lads couldn't do on the football field and those things made me stand out.

I must admit that even at my school there were probably two or three players who were more talented than me, but probably didn't quite have the mentality or the resilience to go on and do more, or maybe they weren't as lucky as me? Luck has a lot to do with how far footballers progress. If you look at Messi and Ronaldo now – and don't get me wrong I am in no way comparing myself to them as they are on a different planet – but it's not just about their talent. How do they still play so well and stay right at the top of their games? Mentality is the key. The ultimate world class players have it and being motivated to carry on is not about money, but the desire to win and the ability never to get into a comfort zone. That can filter down to the rest of us. You must have that same mentality whether it's when making your debut at club level, having a big move, or playing for your country, just as it drove me on.

Yes, I had that 'X-Factor' I guess; I had that electric pace; I could control the ball and run at defenders and I had some skill. I'd always try and play in teams who were above my own age and level; I had no fear-factor playing against people one or two years older than myself – it was a way of testing myself against supposed better, more experienced players. Speed is one thing, but awareness is another - and I had both in abundance. I wasn't just fast, I could read the game well, and that's what set me apart from the rest of the lads in my age group. If I was just a speed merchant, maybe I wouldn't have made it?

Talking about my pace, if I was playing now in the Premier League I would arguably be more protected by referees than when I played. Defenders would try and chop me down and I'd win more free-kicks. Back in the day, I wasn't protected by the referee and defenders would get away with nasty tackles more than they do today. Now you can't even touch a player and the game stops. Not only that, but I'd also probably win more England caps because today's game is all about pace and that was my game. OK, I was up against John Barnes and Chris Waddle, but I was younger than both of those guys.

I don't know where my pace came from; I guess it was natural, maybe it was my build or maybe it came from hours of practice, but nobody could touch me for speed. I used to race against David a lot and although he was very fit, being in the Navy, and probably at his peak, I would always beat him, even though he'd outpace me over the first 20 metres or so. I was so cocky that I'd very often overtake him and beat him every time – sometimes even running backwards in the final 20 metres. That's the one thing that I do remember, Dave! He must have thought I was a freak of nature or something for doing that. However, David always said that my pace came from me having to run away from being disciplined by our mum as a youngster. Not sure about that either! Having said that, it may have been a gene thing because I have a feeling that our mum was a good athlete at her school, so I think that's a more plausible reason for me being a natural athlete. Our father, on the other hand, wasn't sporty at all, but he knew his football and would comment on it as if he knew what he was talking about, even though he'd never kicked a ball in his life.

Something else that I was a natural at was tapdancing – yes, tapdancing. You're probably saying, "Tony Daley, tapdancing? No way!" But to be honest I have a theory that it actually improved my quick feet and dribbling ability as a footballer. Even though it took a while to get into, I eventually enjoyed tapdancing, even though I hated it at first. I actually became good at it. For those who don't know, tapdancing is all about movement and the ability to move your feet around the floor at speed, so my theory that it helped me on the football pitch has some credence, I think. For those who grew up in the 80s, I was in the same dance school as the famous singer/actress Toyah Wilcox.

It all started when I was about seven or eight years old (until I was about 11) and I was introduced to it by my family, who all tap-danced at the local community centre once or twice a week; it was a communal thing and it helped me with my footwork. Not only did I practice but we also put on shows at the Alexandra Theatre and the Hippodrome so I did it to quite a high level.

There was one occasion when I had to choose between competing in a tapdancing competition and playing in a football tournament. Guess which one I chose? Well, there was no way I was going to the tapdancing competition in preference to playing football, even though I got slated for it by our teacher.

From the age of 11, I attended St. George's Comprehensive School so the tap-dancing stopped for two reasons. One, I wanted to concentrate on the football, and secondly, I would have faced loads of banter from the kids at school if I had continued.

St. George's was one of those schools that was famous for churning out an abundance of talented footballers. Apart from myself, there was a list of top players, including Dean Sturridge, Simon Sturridge, Jason Garwood, Rob Alleyne, Carl Garwood, Dave Barnett and going further back, Gordon Cowans. Added to that list, was top speed-skater, Wilf O'Reilly. For such a tiny school (around 600 pupils) it was an awesome achievement.

***

From an early age, I never saw football as being about any one individual; I always saw football as being a team game and that stuck with me throughout my career. That was highlighted when I was about 15 years old and I'd scored 50-odd goals in a season for my Sunday League side Selvey United. At the end of season awards, rather than gloating in the glory of scoring all those goals myself, I honestly wasn't that concerned that I didn't win a trophy; however, I was given a special mention by the coach for my goal scoring exploits and I was well happy with that. From that day on, that was always my outlook on the game, that football was all about your team.

Scoring 50-odd goals at the age of 15, you'd think I was going to be a natural striker later in life, but because of my size (five foot, eight inches) and my speed, I played more on the wing because, as a striker, I was always played out of the game by the big centre-halves, who'd bully me because I had no real physical strength to beat them. On the wing though, I had the speed to skin my man and leave the defenders for dead and I quickly learned to develop my game as a winger. Having said that, a winger in my day was sometimes considered as a 'bonus striker', which probably described the position I eventually played in, so starting off as a striker stood me in good stead. I was probably always going to be a winger though; there were numerous times I'd try a shot at goal and it would end up at the corner flag or fly 50 metres over the bar, so I probably wouldn't have made it as a striker. At school though, I'd very often shoot wildly and the ball very often went over the fence rather than into the top corner of the net. It's a wonder I scored so many goals as a youngster isn't it?

I loved my younger days - even in the school holidays, I'd always be away playing football in tournaments somewhere in the country, unlike a lot of kids now, who'd probably prefer to sit in front of their X-Box than play football. I guess you'd consider it a 'normal' childhood and a lot of you reading this would recognise some of the things I did as a child, some of the games I played and some of the things I went through. I guess I did have a pretty 'normal' upbringing, but sport, and football in particular, was always at the forefront of my mind.

And it didn't do me any harm at all.

I have to mention someone who had a big influence in my early development, my Sunday League manager Ken Wilson. I was playing for fun in those days and never realised my own potential, but Ken obviously did. One day, he saw me play for my district and asked me if I played Sunday league football. At that time, I didn't and only played for my school team. Ken asked me if I fancied playing for a local team called Selvey United, who played in the Birmingham Boys' League. I knew nothing about Sunday league football, so I accepted Ken's invitation after getting approval from my parents. However, approval from my parents wasn't straight forward; they were concerned I already trained on a Thursday and the Sunday league training session was in Barr Beacon, north of Birmingham - probably a good six miles away. Mum and Dad didn't drive at that time, so they were concerned how I'd get there. However, the Selvey coach at the time, Don Link, told Mum and Dad that he would pick me up and bring me back home, which was very kind of him.

With Mum and Dad's approval of the arrangements I started to play for Selvey. Don was great with me, because not only did he drive me to and from home, but he'd also take me to his house before training and his lovely wife would cook for me, before heading off for training. Don would also take me to and from Sunday games.

We had a fantastic team in those days under the management of Ken Wilson. He was an old-fashioned disciplinarian in the mould of Sir Alex Ferguson; he wanted the best for each and every one of his players; his training was superb and we weren't allowed to mess around. Having said that, all our training sessions were enjoyable and that was the main thing. We trained hard, even at such a young age and I'm sure his disciplined ways have rubbed off on me and that has helped me become such a disciplined person myself in later life. Even though Ken was a Birmingham City fan (I won't hold that against him!) I learned such a lot from him and he played a massive part in my development, not only as a footballer, but as a human being. He demanded high standards, on and off the field, and that can only be a good thing for any youngster – it was for me, anyway.

I loved playing for Selvey United; I loved playing football

and I couldn't go a day without playing, so to be able to play in a Sunday league team was perfect for me. The help and support I got from Ken and Don and the players was amazing and they were like a second family to me. They really looked after me. What a wonderful family they were. I will always be truly grateful to them for helping me progress my career.

Although I had trained with Birmingham City and Blackpool, I ended up signing schoolboy forms at Villa at the age of 14. Then, only a couple of years later, I took the next step. I will never forget the day when I received a letter from Villa saying they were going to take me on as a YTS (Youth Training Scheme) – it was an awesome feeling as a 16-year-old who was just about to leave school. As soon as I saw the letter, I wanted to tell all the people who had influenced me during those early years. However, the first thing I did was to tell my parents, of course, and they were so pleased for me. I then told my school PE teacher, Colin Rogers, who really helped my football development in the early days and had a major influence on my career, and I then told Ken Wilson and Don Link.

My Villa heroes at the time were Mark Walters, Gary Shaw, Des Bremner, Gordon Cowans and Allan Evans – it was ironic that not too far into the future, I'd be training with some of those guys.

It was the 'official' start of my football career and the time I was about to fulfil that dream.

It was around that time that I recall going to Villa Park with my brother Euton to watch Villa play Ipswich Town on an April midweek night in 1981, our league title year. Ipswich were neck and neck with Villa for the title and everyone thought whoever won that game would win the title. The stadium was at its capacity if not oversubscribed; we were in the Holte End and the atmosphere was electric. However, it was very difficult to watch the game as we were packed like sardines - I had to climb up on Euton's shoulders to see it! Although gutted we lost the game 2 - 1, results went our way in next few games to take the Division One title. Everyone talks about the high intensity of today's Premier League, but let me tell you, that game against Ipswich was one hell of a game played with incredible pace, strength and skill. It was a pleasure to watch the twin striker combination of Shaw and Withe and the direct pace and dribbling of Tony Morley. As a 14-year-old kid I couldn't wait to get the opportunity to experience this on the field of play.

CHAPTER 2
Making The Break

"My dream finally came true."

BY THE 1982 - 1983 SEASON, Aston Villa were Champions of Europe after beating Bayern Munich 1 – 0 during that famous night in Rotterdam on the 26th May 1982; then they subsequently beat Barcelona in the January of 1983 to lift the European Super Cup, over two legs.

While I can't mention everyone in my youth team group, I would like to talk about a few of the lads who I had some fantastic times with and got on well with. Peter Howell, who came from Aston Manor School and was an apprentice during the 1984 – 1985 season and we used to travel to Bodymoor Heath every day together. The other lads I mixed with were Bernie Gallacher (RIP), a Scottish lad with a wonderful left foot who went on to play for Villa until 1991, Paul Hutchins, Salvatore Vacanti and Paul Granger. Most of the lads I've mentioned, apart from Peter, lived in digs in the Sutton Coldfield area but as we were local, Peter and I lived at home. However, we both caught the bus to meet the other lads at their digs, where we got picked up to be taken to Bodymoor Heath in time for breakfast. This happened five days a week.

I talked about the lads being in digs, well, in those days there used to be maybe four, five or six apprentices sharing the same digs – it must have been cramped to say the least! That simply doesn't happen anymore (thankfully) as an apprentice will have digs to themselves if they are away from home.

Of course, little groups formed within the apprentices and the lads I've just mentioned are the ones I tended to mix with mostly.

It wasn't long after I started as an apprentice – I think I had just turned 16 - that I was playing in the Villa reserve team in the Central League, mixing with the older lads and some reserve and first teamers like Tony Dorigo, Dave Norton, Ray Walker, Dean Glover and Darren Bradley. They were all up-and-coming talents and had either made the first team or were on the verge of making the first team. Not to sound big-headed but I was developing really well and quickly and within two months I was being touted as someone who was good enough to join in with the senior squad myself. Although I was doing well, I had a lot of catching up to do, but I was ready for the challenge. Even at that age, I had no fear; I knew what I could do with the ball; I knew I was good enough to get into the first team, but I wanted to learn off these older lads and I took everything that was said to me on board. It could be said that I was made of steel; I was very humble and happy-go-lucky in that nothing fazed me and I really believe that's a trait all professionals need to possess in order to get to the top.

It was during one of Brian Little's youth-team training sessions that I was asked by the then Villa manager Graham Turner to join the first team setup to fill in during a seven-a-side game as someone had pulled out and they were one man short. I would imagine that Brian had tipped off Graham about me, that I was almost ready to join the first team, but only one step at a time - they obviously didn't want to rush me. I subsequently found out that Graham wanted me to join the first team setup earlier than I actually did, but Brian held me back a bit, although I thought I was ready.

It must be mentioned that even at that stage I was already involved with the England Under 18s and had trained with them several times, so I was a young player who had been mentioned by people outside of Aston Villa as someone who had potential to go far.

During that first taste of first team training, I did everything to impress the rest of the lads and the manager, of course. It was all very well me taking on several first teamers and scoring fancy goals on a small pitch during a seven-a-side game, but to his credit Colin Gibson was quick to tell me it wasn't the same as playing in the first team on a Saturday afternoon.

Brian, as my official coach, told me I could train with the first team for the rest of that week; however, I still wasn't allowed to get changed in the first team dressing room and I still had to do my apprenticeship duties. At the age of 17, I was still doing all the duties an apprentice did back then, like cleaning the pro's boots and sweeping up the dressing room, but I was now training with the first team, a team that consisted of European Cup winners Allan Evans, Colin Gibson, Peter Withe, Gordon Cowans and Nigel Spink, together with seasoned pro's like Steve McMahon, Alan Curbishley and Tony Dorigo. Add to the mix, Mark Walters, Didier Six and Steve Foster – they were just some of the names I had to try and impress and get respect from. I didn't mind doing those chores because it kept me grounded and level-headed. Of course, things are different now and young players probably don't do those jobs.

It really was a surreal period in my career, partly because I was in awe of some of the guys I've just mentioned, they were 'heroes' to me. I used to watch them from the Holte End terraces – I was mixing with them on the training ground. It was mesmerising to say the least. Can you imagine young lads in the Villa academy in 2022 being asked to train with Phillipe Coutinho?

Although I was very young, I also wanted more – a lot more in fact. And right now! I immediately felt comfortable in that environment but I wasn't satisfied playing a bit part, I also understood that I had to wait my turn. It was a dream come true and I wasn't going to let it go!

Incidentally, I had the 'pleasure' of cleaning Steve McMahon's (Macca) boots, who only spent two seasons at Villa, but was considered as a 'hard man' of football in the 1980s. However, I must lift the lid on Steve because his on-field image wasn't the same as the person he really is. I can honestly say that Macca is one of the nicest footballers you'd ever wish to meet; unassuming, quiet and I found it a pleasure and an honour to have cleaned his boots. On the field though he was ruthless. You've probably read about 'old-school' footballers tipping (or not) their boot cleaners at Christmas and I can honestly say that Macca was a very good tipper indeed. It was noticeable that around November time all the first teamers had extremely clean boots, spotless in fact – even cleaner and shinier than usual. I wonder why that was? However, it wasn't just the cleaning of the players' boots that got you a tip. When Christmas was approaching you'd have to face the first teamers and explain why you deserved a tip and very often, the apprentice would be asked to sing a song or tell a joke in the first team dressing room, which was quite a daunting experience, but funny at the same time, mainly at their expense, though.

The first team dressing room has always been a place for jokers, going back to the 1960s and 1970s when footballers were hard and took no prisoners; I've heard stories of youth players or new players coming into the dressing room fold having their socks cut up, clothes torn to shreds and other wind-ups. It all sounded a frightening place to venture into, but I wasn't put off by all those stories.

Mark Walters (Wally) was a player I absolutely idolised at the age of 13 or 14. I remember going to watch him play for the Villa youth team and thinking, "what a player!" His skills, his pace, his composure on the ball. There was a lot of talk about him at the time and I just wanted to be as good as him and he spurred me on to become a wide-player. What I learned the most from him was how direct he was; he'd take defenders on and his first thought was to beat his man, get the ball into the box or to get a shot on target. It was ironic that I followed him into the Villa first team and it was a great feeling to train with him and later on, to play alongside him, as an apprentice. We only played in a handful of first team games together, mainly because we were vying for the same position, but there were a few occasions where we played on opposite wings.

'Wally' always made time for me and gave me some good advice and definitely helped me with my football development. They were big shoes to fill when he left Villa in 1987.

I was happy; I had the opportunity to train with the first team and surprisingly, I found it so relaxing and 'easy' to play with those guys. Football was my passion and back in the 1980s, the dressing room could be a ruthless place; if you didn't have the right personality, the right attitude, the right ability or the combination of all three, you'd get found out. And if that ever happened, you'd get slaughtered and you'd have to learn quickly to adapt, both on and off the field.

In those days, the dressing room was sacrilege; you had to

earn the right to be part of it. As I've mentioned before, I started off not getting changed in the first team dressing room, even though I was training with them, I was nervous even setting foot in the dressing room when Graham (Turner) asked me to go and get so-and-so. I had to knock on the dressing room door and say something like, "The manager wants to speak to Allan Evans." Very often, I was the brunt of the tricksters in the dressing room, with comments like, "Who allowed you in 'ere?"

You were lucky to escape the dressing room fully clothed sometimes, but it was all in the name of good banter.

However, on the pitch they were all good as gold, helping me to improve my game, but in the dressing room they were a different breed. Luckily, nothing fazed me and I learned the 'rules' quickly; there were unwritten rules for a youngster like me to follow, and if you didn't follow them, you were in trouble.

I guess it was all part and parcel of learning my trade and trying to fit in. Obviously, dressing rooms are completely different now and I'd guess none of those shenanigans go on anymore and if they did, there would be trouble, and maybe seen as 'bullying' – someone would probably end up suspended or fined. Sadly, that kind of behaviour isn't accepted now, but at the time it was and didn't do anyone any harm. On the flip side, you could say that the modern-day dressing room is more professional than it used to be and that is a good thing, but the fun has probably disappeared out of it.

Another thing that has changed is when a 16-year-old moves up the ranks into the first team fold now, they most probably think they have "arrived" and their days in the Under-23s are behind them. In my book, their place in the first team must be earned and there isn't a given right to be in the first team dressing room, just because the media are touting them as the next best thing since Gazza. I've always thought it was a privilege to make that step up but regardless of the era, players need to realise they have to earn the right to be there. I was lucky that I had a real good grounding and at no time did I think "I'd arrived", and if I did think like that, I'd have been slaughtered.

Every player who goes through the Villa ranks has ability, no doubt about that – they wouldn't be in there if they didn't have that, but in this day and age, it's not all about ability, it's also about how that player can cope with pressure. It's fine for someone to look like an accomplished player doing tricks and stroking the ball around in an Under-23 game, but it's all about transferring those skills to the first team environment on the big stage in front of 42,000 fans at Villa Park. The other thing is, how will that player cope if and when they have a bad game? Can they handle that? How will they cope with the criticism that comes with the territory? Football managers look at all aspects of a player's game, not just ability, to see how they cope with different experiences. Players need the right mindset and mentality to manage with the change of setting and the step-up in quality of the players that he's playing against. If that player can't produce at the highest level then they won't make it as a modern-day professional footballer. Unfortunately, the reality is that there are lots of young players who look the part in the Under-23 environment but simply haven't got what it takes to reproduce that quality on the big stage; that's a reason why so many footballers simply drop out of the game at a young age, or are moved on to smaller clubs, where they will have less pressure put on them.

One rule I soon learned when I was a youth was never to take the p*** out of a senior pro during training. I still have the scars from Colin Gibson (Gibbo) during a training session, when I picked the ball up, dropped a shoulder and flew past him as if he wasn't there and finally getting a cross into the box. I did this time and time again during small-sided training games; once is fine, but when you continue to do it, that's when the senior pros come after you – they don't like it. Let me tell you, Colin Gibson was a fantastic player and a great guy and we became good friends (and we still are). He was brilliant to play with on that left-hand-side, in that if you didn't do your job on the pitch (or on the training ground) he would tell you in no uncertain way, but when you got the ball and did something good with it, he'd praise you. That's the way you want it to be, black and white.

He was non-stop in your ear for 90 minutes – and I didn't mind that one bit. In fact, I'd rather have a fellow player or manager keep me on my toes than not say anything to me. Playing with Gibbo, there was no comfort zone whatsoever.

However, our friendship didn't start too well. To be fair to Gibbo, he did warn me after the first time and said something like, "Take the p*** out of me again and I'll break your legs." Then he chopped me down with a two-footed tackle – and that was in a training session! He then picked me up, brushed me down and said, "Carry on mate, try that again." That episode taught me a great lesson and it soon told me that the same thing would happen again and again in 'proper' games if I didn't wise up. Those lessons helped give me a ruthless streak I never possessed before, the ability to take players on knowing full well I was going to be taken out, tackled hard from behind, but that never really bothered me. Having said that, it was expected, and it was never meant to be done in anger; however, it was a regular occurrence to see me go down on the training field, merely because no one could catch me and the only thing they could do was to chop me down.

When I had just come into the first team fold, Gibbo offered to do some extra one-on-one training after the main sessions with me. Gibbo took his training seriously, as though it was a game situation and some of the tackles he did on me when I had the ball were ferocious; he didn't want me to take the 'Mickey' out of him when I was doing my 'twinkle-toes' down the wing. Many-a-time I'd beat him for pace and the lads would give Gibbo some stick which he didn't like. Gibbo subsequently became my ally because every time I got whacked during games, he was the one who would say, "Don't worry lad, keep running at them." Before I knew about it, he would clean that player out in the next tackle. That was the time I knew my teammates respected me and were protecting me. It was part and parcel of football in the 1980s. Gibbo told me I'd get a lot of that sort of treatment during games and advised me not to react to it because they would only do it more and more. I wasn't the sort of player who would roll around the ground as if I'd been shot, so that wasn't a problem for me and I would always be one-up on them. The idea of players going in hard in those days was to put the player out of action, to hurt you. There was no pussy-footing about back then.

Footballers in the 1980s not only had strength in their heart, but they had strength in their head that led to most of them having good character, something that is generally lacking from today's game I feel. Football is not only about the physical side, but that mental strength taught us to cope in pressure situations on the pitch. There's a lot of interaction with sports science these days, but while that is all good, it goes out of the window somewhat when players are put under pressure on the pitch.

I was never mouthy on the pitch; I just tried to let my football skills do the talking and with that attitude I quickly gained the respect of the first team players around me. They realised I wasn't talking the p*** and that I actually had ability to hold my own on the pitch; they soon realised they had a wonderful asset amongst their ranks.

As I've said before, I have always loved training and we had to do a lot of running, which was great for me, but some of the lads (most of them) hated it. It was usual for us to start off doing three laps of the Bodymoor Heath training ground in 12 minutes, which was a major run and a tough one, too. I remember completing it and resting up for a couple of minutes while I was waiting for some of the other lads who struggled to finish in the allocated time. Again, that didn't go down too well with some of the senior pros, but they soon realised I wasn't taking the p*** and that I actually enjoyed running and I wanted to succeed as a player in that team. I didn't care when they kept saying, "Stop taking the p***, lad." I just carried on running.

Training was fairly 'old-school' back in the early 1980s, especially pre-season training. We'd always do lots of running up and down hills in the Tamworth area, near to the Bodymoor Heath training ground. The usual routine was running in the morning, back to Bodymoor for lunch, then more running around the training ground in the afternoon. I have to say it was horrible in some ways. You'd very often see people being sick. There was none of the drink breaks to rehydrate that players these days have – we had to do as we were told and put up with the physical and mental fatigue we felt. The word 'hydration' and 'rehydration' weren't in football coaches' vocabularies back then; drinking water was seen as a weakness.

At times, I thought I'd signed up for the Armed Forces, let alone a football team, it was that hard! We were pushed to the very limits, but in hindsight, I can see the relevance of it in a way, in that it gave you strength and character that you needed when you went out to play 90 minutes on a Saturday afternoon; it was almost ingrained into you. Football training has come a long way since then and that's only a good thing.

Looking back, I really don't think half of the guys I played with would have made it through 90 minutes without that daily grind and having that mental resilience. It was only because of that most of us could deal with playing football. When I look back at some of the players we had at the club at that time, Paul McGrath, Gordon Cowans and Peter Withe, those players could drink 10 pints of Guinness the night before a game but would still be streets ahead of everybody else on matchday; they'd had years and years of grounding and set the foundation. I sometimes wonder, how much better they would have been if they had lived their lives the 'right' way. Maybe, physically they would have been even fitter (even though they were super-fit anyway), but mentally, they were resilient. You'd think by picking a few guys out is unfair, but that was the 'norm'; all teams had players who'd drink to excess, eat steak and chips the night before, but come Saturday afternoon, they would perform to the highest level. Tell me a fitter player in today's Premier League than Gordon Cowans was in his prime – he would have stood the test of time and could have easily fitted into any modern team in the Premier League.

Only a few years later, in 1996, Arsène Wenger became Arsenal manager and changed the philosophy of the game in this country forever.

My first pre-season as a pro was when I earned the right to be part of the first team dressing room and it was full of incident. The one occasion I recall most of all was when my car broke down; the clutch had packed in and I was going to be late for my first training session. As I hadn't even left home I phoned the training ground and spoke to Jim Paul, the Villa kitman, and told him I was going to be late in. Jim told me he would come and pick me up and bring me into training, so about half-an-hour later he pulled up outside my house in the gaffer's car. Jim then told me to drive the gaffer's car into Bodymoor Heath while he stayed with my car to wait for the breakdown services to attend. So, there I was, an 18-year-old kid driving Graham Turner's Jaguar! It wasn't the start I wanted, nor did it set a good example to the new manager, being late for the first day of pre-season training. If I recall, no damage was done once I arrived at Bodymoor Heath.

I won't lie, but I found youth football really easy; the more I was pushed, the more I enjoyed it - the higher the level I went, the more I enjoyed it, too. I had the ability to cope with being pushed by my coaches. Brian Little was my youth team coach at Villa and I learned so much from him. He had just retired from the game in 1981 and was given a chance to be a coach at Villa under Graham Turner, so I had a master as a coach.

Brian Little will always be a Villa legend and him coaching me was something special. One thing I won't ever forget was when Brian gave me a gift, a little Buddha charm. He gave it to me because I was going through a bad spell and he told me to take the Buddha, keep it for one season and take it out with me every time I played. So, I took Brian's advice and decided to tuck the little charm in with my socks when I was playing and in my bag when I was in transit. Low and behold, I took it everywhere I went and that season I was on fire; I never forgot to take that Buddha anywhere I went. If I remember rightly, I passed it onto my brother the following year.

That was the season that the first team coaches started to take notice of me, so I owe a lot to Brian's kindness and faith in me at a young age. Not only is Brian a kind and considerate guy, but he also gave me loads of advice when I worked with him. He told me not to fear anything, the 'no-fear factor' as he called it; he told me I was in the first team because what I was doing was good and I deserved to be in the team. He told me not to do anything less or anything more. He knew I had a God-given talent to knock the ball and run 10 yards past a defender and he wasn't the only person to tell me I didn't have to do fancy turns or flicks. In other words, "be who you are and try not to be anyone different – on and off the field."

I think Brian improved me as a young player no-end, not only with his advice but his calming nature helped to settle me down. I can't remember any time Brian shouted at me (or anyone else for that matter), which doesn't mean to say he wasn't disciplined, because he was, but you would never find him screaming and balling at anyone. I really think I related to his calming nature and it made me a lot more positive about doing stuff. For instance, if I did something wrong on the pitch, Brian would have a more positive effect on me than someone who screamed at me. The screaming coach wouldn't get a response from me but the way Brian went about his business had the opposite effect. Brian always seemed on the same level as his players – there was never any aloofness about him, probably because he hadn't long retired as a player himself.

Having watched Brian play for Villa I had the upmost respect for him as well; I couldn't believe he was my youth team coach – I was a bit in awe of him if I'm honest and still am – but don't tell him that! Brian treated me as if I was the best player in the team. I aspired to be someone like him and he helped me to improve my game so much that I felt I was the best player on the pitch.

Graham Turner was always very good with me too. He once said to me, "Take your chances when you can," and that is something that always stuck in my head. He was right of course because you normally only get one chance to prove yourself in football. He also said, "Never change your style or the way you play because that's why you're training with the first team." He obviously liked the way I played and urged me not to change my style. Given these were the days when there was no consistency between the way the youth teams played and the way the first team played (unlike what it is now where all the setups play the same way), Graham was telling ME to play the same way as I did in the youth team, which was refreshing. Although most teams played 4-4-2 or a variant of that system, it was easy for me to adjust to life in the first team. I either found myself on the right or left-wing, getting into the box on the end of crosses or helping the full-backs out. It was a very simple game back then. I was told that when I picked the ball up to always give the defender a torrid time. Graham knew I had the pace and he always told me to knock the ball past the defender and run; there was no need for me to do fancy tricks. He always said if there was the space it wasn't a bad thing if you were quicker than the defender to run past him. That, in itself, was a trick.

I offered something quite different to Villa; there weren't too many players in the side who were lightning quick as I was – if anyone at all. Someone with pace would always excite the crowd and that was my job.

Graham as a person was a quiet individual but I had full respect for him as my manager. You could say he was an 'old-school' type of manager. He was very disciplined and training sessions were a time for us to work and not mess about; afterwards, we could do what we liked (to a certain extent), but during his time, we had to be focused on training. We also had fun and always joked in the dressing room; Graham didn't want a dressing room full of robots but he demanded that we concentrate on our training while we were on duty. When he spoke to you as an individual he was constructive and concise with his instructions; you knew exactly what he wanted from you, which for me as a young player was just what I needed. If you weren't doing your job, you knew about it. It wasn't the case of him telling you that you'd done something wrong and not following up on what you'd done wrong; he would go into some detail about the mistakes you'd made and how to do things differently. That's what I mean by constructive. Some managers just fling comments at you, that you've done something wrong and then move on, but Graham was actually worth listening to and gave you some encouragement to improve yourself. Being able to speak to a manager face-to-face on a one-to-one basis, was for me far better than a manager who only communicates to the group or is aloof.

The style of football Graham liked to play was what some may call 'long ball' but that was typical of the day. He liked his teams to play to their strengths and we were no different, having two wide players to cross into the big target man up top.

As a general rule, I liked managers who kept me on my toes; I hated receiving mixed messages from managers, but Brian, Graham Turner, and later Graham Taylor, were clear in their communication, so I knew exactly what they wanted from me. When I talk about 'mixed messages' I mean, for example, if I thought I hadn't played well and a manager said to me, "Well done today," I'd interpret that as him not being quite sure about me or not being quite truthful – whereas someone like Brian would have said to me something like, "You could have done better doing (this or that)," and he'd give me a number of reasons and suggestions on how I could do something better or differently. Conversely, if I played well, Brian would say something like, "You played well today. You did (this or that) well." If I didn't play well, I always knew it, so for someone to tell me "Well done today," when I knew I hadn't, was wrong in my book. I'd always trust what a manager said when the message was constructive and not just a fly-by comment.

Brian also taught me something when I was 18 or 19 that

I kept in my locker for the whole of my professional football career. Before he became the youth team coach, I used to read the match reports in the newspapers and, to be honest, took what I read as gospel. For example, if the local Birmingham pink sports paper (*Sports Argus*) scored me four out of 10, I'd take it personally and it would stick with me for the rest of the week; it would wind me up. Brian told me not to take anything from second-hand reports and only listen to him as my coach. If I played badly, there were always things that we could do to improve my game during the week. Reading some of the reports I sometimes wondered if the journalist was at the same game because very often my coach would give me the opposite feedback that didn't match the newspaper report. Very often I'd read reports that just because a player scored the winner, he'd get a nine but someone who did his job and didn't put a foot wrong only got a five. To me, it didn't make any sense at all. I soon learned not to read those reports, or if I did, it would go over my head and I didn't let it get to me, so I could go into training the following week on an even keel.

I really think if I took those newspaper reports to heart it would have affected my future career. Fortunately, there was no social media in the 1980s and 1990s – and I really mean that, so we had no distractions that the players of today have; all we had were newspapers, TV and radio, so thank God we didn't have the side-shows players face now, with fans and keyboard warriors slating players, managers and teams after every poor performance (or good one). People often ask me how would I cope with social media if I was a player nowadays? As someone who is a lot wiser than I was when I played the game, I'd have interacted with the fans and I would say it's a good thing – if used in the right way. Yes, it can be dangerous at times, especially if players start arguing with fans and things get out of hand. I really think I'd interact with fans whether I had a good game or not. Social media gives the fans access to players and I would have embraced that, to a certain extent.

Unfortunately, there are too many idiots out there who spoil it for others. In my view, the vast majority of fans I interact with are good and truthful. I'm all in favour of constructive criticism, especially if a player hasn't played well, but when it becomes personal, then that's where the lines are drawn. Unfortunately, racism, sexism and other online abuse now exist – it did in my day, but now it's all out in the open. Due to social media there is a lot more access to people than there ever was before. Also, people seem to have a lot more to say for themselves now. If I'm honest, if I was a young player I would report any abuse I came across and as an advocate of anti-racism I do report any instances I come across on social media. Like anything, social media has its good bits and bad bits but I think 99.5% of people on social media are decent.

One thing that is for sure, racism is completely different to what it was when I was a player. I will speak more about my views and experiences of racism later in the book, but I'll just say this; while I'm talking about social media, just imagine if we had social media in the 1980s, when racism was 'accepted' and seen as 'banter' on the terraces and there were next to no consequences from it. It would be a completely different environment altogether; at least there is awareness and consequences now, but back then there was ignorance and bad behaviour was 'tolerated' to a certain extent.

I've heard people say that footballers (and other high-profile professionals) shouldn't be on social media because they leave themselves wide open for abuse. Well, I can see that point but I think the opposite and I'll tell you why. Back in the day, I could go into my local shop and say hello to anyone in the shop, sign a few autographs and have a chat but players of today can't do that. Imagine someone like Jack Grealish going into his local supermarket – he'd be mobbed. Footballers these days, especially the high-profile ones, can't interact with fans like we did; some obviously do on a small scale and sometimes I see pictures on social media of a fan pictured in a shop with a player, but these occurrences are becoming few and far between.

I will always recall after one particular game I played in, coming out of Villa Park with my young daughter who was screaming and balling, trying to get her into my car; I just wanted to get in the car and go home, but I managed to spend 10 minutes signing autographs before jumping in the car. Then, a day or so later, someone had written in the local newspaper that I'd ignored him and called me "an absolute disgrace." When I read that it upset me because I don't remember ignoring anyone that Saturday afternoon – I would never do anything like that anyway. That was the worst I had and I was fine with that, but just imagine if that same thing happened now, with mobile phones everywhere and social media? I'd be strung up on social media for apparently "ignoring" a fan.

So, there are my reasons why players should use social media to interact with fans – to a certain extent anyway. When interactions start getting out of hand, then is the time to stop. I think clubs should include clauses in contracts about social media interactions, where penalties exist if that player breaks protocol. On the other hand, players should be taught how to use social media properly. Facebook, Instagram and Twitter can become good tools if used properly.

I don't see any harm in players being responsible, showing off their cars or showing pictures of themselves on the beach in the right context; they earn that money so why shouldn't they show it off, not in a flashy way, but in the right context? The problem comes when people take exception to this type of media and they start the jealous abuse and the player wades in with a reaction. That's when the player steps out of line. It's all about getting the balance right and about education, what's right and acceptable and what's not.

The relationship between footballers and managers and journalists is something else that has changed over the years. Once, you could say things 'off the record' but now, that hardly ever happens for fear of being 'stitched up'. The latter part of my career was the start of a period of mistrust of journalists, where they would mis-interpret a story that was given to them. I had some experiences that led me to distrust a journalist or two so I ended up not saying anything to them, or giving them the standard talk, which was a shame. It seems that all some journalists of today want are more social media followers, given the headlines they spin. All it takes is a story to get out of hand and that journalist will quickly cut off the hand that fed him; other players won't talk to that journalist so he is the one who loses out in the end.

***

I'd only been training with the first team squad for a matter of weeks, training with some of the remaining 1982 European Cup winning team, when I suddenly announced myself by beating a number of players and scoring a terrific goal in training. From that piece of brilliance, the other players suddenly started to take notice of me. I will always remember Brian Little saying to me, "Do what you're supposed to do." So, I did. That was the training session that I've already mentioned, where Colin Gibson chopped me down and told me not to take the p***. That tackle cleaned me out but I made sure it didn't hurt me and just carried on. In fact, it kept happening, Gibbo kept chopping me down, and I kept getting up, brushed myself down and carried on without a word. I think I quickly earned the respect of the senior players by not moaning about the hard tackles that were flying in. I wasn't scared and it quickly taught me that senior football was so much harder than youth team football.

I also recall Martin Keown wanting to do some extra training with me so I could improve my crossing and for him to improve his heading, which goes to show that the senior players had seen something in me that they liked and wanted to help me mature as a player. This then became a regular occurrence, maybe once or twice a week for 20 or 30 minutes after training. What I did was to run down the touchline and fizz some balls into the box and Martin would clear it away or head the ball into the empty net. Martin made it clear it was HIS training session, but he did allow me to practice my heading as well, which was good for me as heading was the weakest part of my game. It wasn't just the case of pinging the ball into the box, I had to dribble around cones.

I hated heading the ball – some people would say it would mess up my hair do, but Martin would use the time to practice clearing the ball so I could jump and head the ball towards goal. Martin gave me some good advice regarding heading the ball. I learned it was all about timing but I didn't practice enough, even though I had a decent leap on me, which was good for those flick-ons. Heading wasn't my strength so those sessions really helped my game. As a player, I always did extra training and it was usually something different every day. I wanted to improve my overall game. I'd usually call upon a full-back, a centre-back, a goalkeeper and a striker to help with the sessions. Every session included me running at people with the ball, some fancy tricks and letting fly with a cross.

A few years later, when Graham Taylor had become manager, he pulled me up, pointed in front of me and said, "What's that in front of you?" I looked at him bewilderingly as all I could see was grass. He asked, "What's your party piece?"

To which I said, "Well, I can do a stepover like Mark Walters."

It wasn't the answer he wanted to hear, "If you knock the ball past the player and run past them, there's not many people who can do that and give people two yards and get past them. Use that, don't be afraid because that is a trick. Use that space and run at the defenders." He told me to knock the ball and run. He used the term 'slow trigger', which meant first thinking about what I wanted to do and controlling the cross on the run. He went on, "When you get into that position and you're running at 100mph, you've got the ball and a defender breathing down your arse behind you, slow your mind down and release the trigger." After he gave me that piece of information, I did just that – I remembered the 'slow trigger' when I was in that position with the ball at my feet and I was about to cross the ball.

I couldn't get enough of it and I loved it.

The more I trained the more I was accepted – and the more I felt ready!

I also felt comfortable with the group of players I was working with. I had no fear – I just wanted to play football. To me, it seemed a natural progression to make. I was growing up fast and this was another part of me maturing.

It was like I was destined to play for Aston Villa. I had no alternative, although my mum would say she had a 'Plan B' for me and that's why I did well in my education in the end. I did start doing an accountancy course at night-school when I was 16 but that quickly stopped once I had a foot in the door at Bodymoor Heath. However, in the back of my mind I did have a 'Plan B' of my own, but more about that later. I was more obsessed with football and I was obsessed with getting into the Villa first team. I always knew football was a short career so I was always going to make the most of my talents and make sure I got into the first team at an early stage of my life. And that's exactly what happened.

Those who know me will say I'm not arrogant, quite the opposite in fact, but I felt I'd arrived at that point. Everyone who plays football at that level has to have faith in their own ability and at that time in my career I was feeling on top of the world and ready to show people what I was all about. A few years previously, I had a dream about playing for Aston Villa and for England and told everyone who would listen that I would do everything in my power to achieve those goals, so that day was the start of it all. It wasn't about the money in those days, the money wasn't great – it was more about playing football and being the best at it.

There were a couple of friendlies that I was asked to go to, but wasn't involved in, just to make up the numbers and to get me adjusted to the first team environment more than anything, prior to finding myself in the squad in a testimonial game against Bristol Rovers. It was the first time I'd been recognised by Graham Turner, the Villa manager at the time. He started me at Eastville and I had a brilliant game. I was only 16 and a couple of months into my apprenticeship at the club. It was also the first time that the press noticed me and they began to ask who this 'wonderkid' was. That game gave me the springboard and confidence to improve.

Shortly after the Bristol Rovers game I was promoted to training with the reserves and also trained fairly frequently with the first team. It wasn't until April when I travelled down with the first team to Southampton that I was told by Graham Turner that I was playing in the game at The Dell (the old Southampton ground). I thought I was doing 'kit' duties with Jim Paul, our kitman! I had no time to think about it, no time to worry about it, not that I ever worried about playing. I was about to start my football career. That day was 20th April 1985 and I wore the number eight shirt. It was a day I will never forget, although we lost the game 2 – 0. Nerves never played any part of my game; once I got onto the football field, any butterflies disappeared and I did what I had to do. That day was quite an experience because I played against the great ex-England full-back Mick Mills, who retired at the end of that season. I'm not sure if playing against me had anything to do with it! Incidentally, an ageing Jimmy Case, who was still as hard as nails, and my future Villa teammate Andy Townsend, also played for Southampton that day.

I was only 17 when I made my debut and still living with my parents but I must have made an impression in the local area as I had a steady stream of visitors at our door who wanted my autograph. Being the proud mum she was, nobody was left disappointed. It's hard to imagine that sort of thing happening to young footballers nowadays. My mum was proud as punch that her son was playing for the Villa first team and the one thing she instilled in me was that I should please the fans and make them appreciate me by taking time out to have a chat with everyone of them. My mum knew that the fans were important and made me stop what I was doing when someone knocked on the door, even if I was in the middle of something, "No, Tony, you come now – they're waiting for you."

The attendances were low in the mid-1980s, and not just at Villa Park, partly because of the game losing its place in society a bit. Football was going through a 'transitional' phase and the attendances were falling due to the concerns over the onset of hooliganism and poor stadium facilities, added to the perceived poor quality shown on the pitch. There was a sense of gloom abounding in the domestic game at the time, although English clubs still did well in Europe. Of course, I wasn't concerned about what was going on off the field, I just wanted to make the people who were watching on the terraces go home happy and give them some entertainment during those 90 minutes on the pitch.

From memory, my home debut was in the next game, a draw against Watford in front of only 11,493, then against QPR where we won 5 – 2. I missed out in the home victory against Sunderland but was substitute against Luton, coming on late in the second-half and started in the last game of the season defeat against Liverpool. I think my family were watching in the stands for that last game, so I felt very proud to be playing in front of them. As a Villa fan, walking out on the hallowed turf of Villa Park as a young, fresh-faced youth was something I will never forget. My dream came true. This is what I wanted to do more than anything. I wanted to do so well on the pitch but I had that nervous apprehension before every game, and especially every time I went out at Villa Park.

Liverpool were the dominant side in English football back then and several times I managed to get past Alan Hansen and head to the edge of the box only to be fouled. I could hear the excitement in the crowd, the Villa fans getting up on their feet to watch this unknown young player try and get round the solid

Liverpool defence. It's funny recapping those early days, because I remember the silence in the crowd when I picked the ball up and started running down the wing; the anticipation amongst the Villa faithful, then as soon as I started to run with the ball, they would get up on their feet and I could hear the clatter of the old wooden chairs followed by the buzz of the crowd. It was a thrill for me to create such an excitement amongst the fans every time I got the ball. I sensed that buzz every time I played thereafter, and it became almost expected of me that I would take on two or three players and race into the box. In some respects, that buzz I created kind of made me want to do more and work harder for those fans. Conversely, if I mis-controlled the ball or a pass went astray I would sometimes hear individual voices expressing their disquiet (or vitriol) but I soon learned to ignore those voices. Those voices were clear as daylight when I played in the reserves, in front of maybe a handful of hardened fans, "Come on Daley, what the f*** was that?"

I featured in five games as a 17-year-old, more than I'd ever expected if I'm honest. As an apprentice and playing in the youth team I was on £25-per-week, and when I stepped up to play in the first team I'd get bonuses. I got something like £250 for a win, £100 a draw on top of £250 appearance money. So, for the first five first team games I earned a whopping £250 appearance bonus on top of my £25-a-week apprenticeship wage. Unfortunately, I only appeared in one game out of the five that we won so I earned another £250 for that game. For me, that added up to a lot of money, more money than I'd ever seen before.

Although the start of my career was full of ups and downs, I did enough in those five games to earn my first professional contract and signed a four-year deal worth a whopping £150-a-week, increasing by £150-a-week every year. When I told my mum about my contract and how much I would be earning she said, "You won't see £150 a week." Meaning I'd have to pay my way. Even so, I still felt like 'Jack the Lad' earning what was, in those days, a decent wage for a 17-year-old.

Although money wasn't my main motivator in those days, signing that deal meant a lot to me and the money came in handy.

For Villa, and for Graham Turner the 1984 – 1985 season saw no improvement to the previous season where the club had finished 10th under Tony Barton, with a side consisting of mainly the backbone of the European Cup winning squad. What could I expect from the next season, hopefully my first full season as a professional footballer?

My elder brother, David, used to drive me to and from the ground when I started playing in the first team, even though I'd just passed my driving test. He used to drop me off outside the ground which meant driving through Witton Lane which was blocked to the public on matchdays. I used to rock up at the ground early, maybe an hour and half before kick-off. So, one day David dropped me off as usual but this time the police officer wouldn't let us through the barricaded road, so I gave him the 'do you know who I am?' treatment, telling him that I was playing today. The officer didn't recognise me and said, "I don't care if you're playing." He wouldn't let us go any further, so I got out of the car and walked the rest of the way to the stadium.

We played Liverpool at home in the second game of the 1985 1986 season and I came on as a substitute. That Liverpool side consisted of players like Kenny Dalglish, Phil Neal, Alan Hansen, Mark Lawrenson and Ian Rush. It was a team who were to go on and do the domestic double that season. Here I was, a skinny 17-year-old in his sixth appearance in the first team coming on and immediately making his mark. It didn't take me long to show the Champions-elect who I was and what I could do when I picked the ball up and took on Hansen and Lawrenson as if they weren't there. It was only a last-ditch tackle that prevented me from scoring. It was a moment I will never forget, not only did I nearly score but I remember the Villa crowd fell silent when I got the ball and started running past these experienced defenders in red. Apparently, I was the talk of Villa Park – that run was the highlight of the game and I was being talked about by the faithful. Although we narrowly lost that game, it was probably the game that announced Tony Daley to the Villa fans. It was a very significant game for me and my career.

I think I made the substitutes bench for the next game but then started against QPR, Luton and West Bromwich Albion. My first senior goal came in my fifth appearance of the season, away to

The Baggies. We won that game 3 – 0 and I scored our second goal. Unfortunately, that game wasn't televised and for the life of me, I can't find any video footage on YouTube, which is a shame because it was an absolute screamer. I picked the ball up 40 yards out, ran past a couple of players and then hit the ball from 25 yards out and the ball rocketed past the 'keeper into the top corner of the net. I just can't describe the feeling of scoring my first goal for Villa – wow! It was just like scoring a goal in the playground at school. In fact, I practiced that goal a million times at William Cowper School in the playground against a brick wall and to actually score THAT goal at the Hawthorns was unbelievable.

I didn't really practice celebrations – it wasn't the thing we did back then, not like now, when goal celebrations are a big thing, but it didn't turn out how I imagined it. However, in terms of how it felt at the time, it was everything I wanted it to be and more.

That was the goal I will always remember the most – everyone remembers their first goal, don't they?

My first team career was beginning to blossom and more people were getting to know my name.

I started 16 games and made seven substitute appearances in the league during that first season and scored two goals. I struggled towards the middle to end of that 1985 – 1986 season with a pain in my pubis and I was in and out of the side from January 1986 onwards, playing just a handful of games.

***

It was a transitional season for the club, where a lot of the 'old guard' were leaving or had left, including Dennis Mortimer, Peter Withe, Des Bremner, Eamon Deacy, Colin Gibson, Brendon Ormsby and Steve McMahon. In came players like Steve Hodge, Paul Elliott and Simon Stainrod. Brian Little also left his post as youth team coach during the season. Although I didn't play, I remember our lowest crowd for three decades at Villa Park – only 8,456 turned up to watch a goalless draw against Southampton. Times were hard – it was hard enough watching from the stands let alone playing.

We finished 18th in the league, although we managed to reach the semi-final of the League Cup, only to be knocked out by Oxford United. However, I didn't feature in any of the latter rounds of the cup. We languished around the relegation zone for most of that season but won three from the last five games to save our season. It was only what we deserved.

We all knew we needed a strong start to the 1986 – 1987 season but what followed was a horror show. The problems were there for all to see from the end of the first game at home to Spurs. A Clive Allen hat-trick was the sign of things to come, as he had no problem breaching our defence.

With the players we had at the club, we were expected to have done better than the previous season; the team was full of potential. However, our problems were in defence. Martin Keown and Tony Dorigo were only 20 and Paul Elliott and Dave Norton weren't much older. The experienced Allan Evans also featured for the first half of the season. Our midfield was talented, with Steve Hodge already an England regular, Paul Birch (Birchy), Steve Hunt, Mark Walters and Neale Cooper, as well as myself. On paper we had a decent frontline, with Gary Thompson, Andy Gray and Simon Stainrod, but all three under-performed that season. As I say, our defence leaked goals, and at an alarming rate – two or more goals per game on 23 occasions during that season.

I seem to remember our chairman, Doug Ellis, giving Graham the dreaded 'vote of confidence' after the defeat to Oxford, stating that the team were suffering from three key absences, but no one could support Graham after the embarrassing trip to Nottingham Forest, which saw us lose heavily by 6 – 0. That was the final straw. As a Villa fan it wasn't what I wanted to see, but I had started to establish myself as a first team player so for me, it was doubly disappointing to see us lose five out of six games at the start of the season. We were in trouble and so was Graham Turner. He desperately wanted to be a success but it ended up being a disaster.

Doug Ellis did what he had to do and that was terminate Graham's contract after that humiliating defeat. Ron Wylie took temporary charge. Ron was our youth team coach, replacing Brian at the start of 1986 and he was a really decent man indeed. He was an experienced coach but, unfortunately, he couldn't stop the rot, as we were tortured by Norwich in his first and only game in charge.

On 22nd September, in came Manchester City manager,

Billy McNeill, after resigning from his post at Maine Road to become Villa manager. He came in with a big reputation, not least for being the captain of the 'Lisbon Lions', the Celtic team who won the European Cup in 1967. He'd had success at Celtic as a manager, winning five trophies in five seasons and got Manchester City promoted in 1984 – 1985. Big things were expected of him at Villa Park.

One of his first tasks was to try and stop Steve Hodge from leaving the club. Hodgey was eager to leave the sinking ship and by December he'd gone to Tottenham. However, McNeill's biggest issue was to stop the lack of discipline on and off the pitch. One thing I remember about McNeill at that time was the utter lack of control he seemed to have with the players. That said, to me he couldn't handle the big characters in the dressing room. There was a big drinking culture at the club, which as I've mentioned before, was alien to me as I was tee-total. It seemed McNeill had no influence on (or off) the training field and the players were showing a complete lack of respect for him. All those nights out on the pop took its toll and the result was shown on the pitch.

At first, it looked like McNeill had worked wonders, as we drew 3 – 3 at Anfield and then won four out of the next five. By that time, I hadn't scored all season but did in the defeat at Maine Road. That defeat seemed to spell danger for the rest of that season, as we only took 12 points from 60. Things only got worse. A fate was sealed after a 2 – 1 defeat at home to Sheffield Wednesday. I wore the number 11 shirt that day and all I remember was seeing a wall of police officers and stewards lining the perimeter of the pitch to try and prevent a pitch invasion from the 15,000 dissatisfied Villa fans.

Billy McNeill didn't even see out the season as he was sacked before the last game of the season, an away trip to Old Trafford. Frank Upton took charge and that game ended in yet another defeat.

Doug Ellis was looking for his fourth manager in three torrid years. In fact, we'd actually had four different managers during that season, if you include Ron Wylie and Frank Upton, who only took charge for one game each.

We were no longer a top-tier club and had to plan for life in Division Two.

CHAPTER 3
Graham Taylor: My Football Father

"Graham Taylor was the best manager for my football career."

GRAHAM TAYLOR came into Villa Park during the summer of 1987, fresh from leading Watford to a semi-final defeat in the 1986 FA Cup and was appointed to get Villa back into the First Division (before the Premier League) after being relegated under Billy McNeill.

Graham had come to a club that were at rock-bottom and had all sorts of problems. Villa had tumbled out of Division One for the first time in nearly three decades. Football in those days had problems too; there was a drinking culture in every club, including Villa, and players were just starting to earn half-decent money, even though it wasn't great. There was a night-club culture too, during a time when footballers were slowly becoming mini-celebrities. For me, we were relegated because the players didn't do enough and I include myself in that. I was always committed to the cause, being a Villa fan, I felt I had something else, but I didn't think some of my teammates had enough commitment to the club. Add that to the lack of discipline there was at the club, where players weren't challenged about their behaviour off the field, then you had a disaster waiting to happen – and it happened!

Graham Taylor's reign at the club couldn't have come any sooner for me. I wasn't one to hang out at night clubs. I didn't drink alcohol so that drinking culture passed me by, but unfortunately, most of the lads frequented the pubs and clubs around Birmingham all too often.

Having said that, things didn't start too well. I think it was about four or five days into Graham's reign that he first spoke to me. I never even heard him call out my name in training. As someone who'd been at the club from a very young age, I was quite shocked at that. I even walked past him one day in a corridor, tried to catch his eye, but he walked straight past me. I thought to myself, "f****** hell, I've got no chance here." I started to think my days were numbered. It was quite daunting and put me on the back foot a little bit. It was a really strange period of my career.

However, Graham eventually called a meeting with all the players and he spelled out his rules and what he expected of us as players on and off the field. I remember him telling us as a group, "You're either with me or you can leave." He told us that it would be tough. From that very first meeting, I knew it was going to be the hardest pre-season we've ever had and it would be a hard season for us. Graham wasn't going to take any prisoners, you either did what you were told and went along on the journey, or you'd be booted out. You could tell Graham liked a disciplined camp and brought in some rules that surprised some of the lads. No one was allowed to wear jeans or shorts around the training ground; it wasn't the case of coming to training in a suit, merely dressed smartly (no jeans) and to a certain standard. The word 'standard' was part of Graham's philosophy. He deplored lateness and imposed fines for anyone who turned up at Bodymoor Heath late or not on time for the coach on matchdays. Not only fines, but he didn't rule out dropping players for ill-discipline.

The other thing Graham disliked was players going out drinking until the late hours. As I've said before, we had a drinking culture in the club and during one early meeting I had with him he told me to disassociate myself with the drinkers, even though I didn't drink myself. I think he thought they would be a bad influence on me. It was one thing Graham was going to weed out – the drinking culture. He wasn't against players enjoying themselves, but he didn't like the players drinking to excess and it affecting their training.

Those two early meetings with Graham were, in hindsight, a test of character and for him to see where I was – whether I was a disciplined footballer or someone who wanted to abuse his position as a professional player.

Talking about the 'drinking culture', we had a Players' Lounge where the old Traveller's Club building was in the old Trinity Road stand. This place was like heaven to most of the players who drank because it was a free bar so you can imagine the fun and games that went on there, after every home game. Some people would spend the whole day in there getting legless – some probably missed the game as well! Amongst those who were allowed into the Players' Lounge were, not only players and their guests, but celebrities and I certainly remember people like Nigel Kennedy and the lads from Take That going in there. A few years later, probably around 1991, one celebrity moment that sticks out for me was when Kevin Kennedy (Curly Watts from Coronation Street) came in after a game with one of the Manchester clubs. He was a big celebrity in those days and everybody knew of him. When he came in, I remember he looked as though he had a 'hydration problem' already! He came over to talk to us and took a liking to my two-month-old baby daughter, Sheridan, and insisted on holding her in the air but then when he took her it looked as though he juggled Sheridan in the air and nearly dropped her. The whole room fell silent as they looked on at an embarrassed Kevin. Luckily, someone was able to rescue Sheridan as quickly as possible and she was unharmed and placed back in my arms. I believe the Villa official photographer Terry Weir actually took a picture of it.

The Players' Lounge was the place where footballers and staff would go after the game and chat with the opposition, so in those days, I'd be speaking with players like with Klinsmann, Beckham and Gascoigne (Gazza). What I liked was going into a battle on the pitch at 3pm on a Saturday afternoon and maybe I'd been involved in a horrendous tackle, some scuffling or swearing, but come 5pm, everything had been forgotten and I'd be chatting to these guys as if nothing had happened. It was a great place to socialise and to wind down. Never did the battles on pitch spill over into the Players' Lounge. Well, I didn't see any, but there could have been over the years.

There are other stories from the Players' Lounge but what went on in the Players' Lounge stayed in the Players' Lounge. That story about Kevin Kennedy was just a taster as it involved me.

***

So, here I was, a 19-year-old 'wonder kid' who'd established himself in the first team for nearly two years, feeling that this manager didn't fancy me as a player. I'd always been encouraged by previous managers and coaches; I'd never had any negative comments made against me and people always told me that I was a very good player with a bright future. Suddenly I was blanked and felt as if I was about to be turfed out. I didn't really know what to make of the meeting but it shocked me a bit. Graham was blunt and to the point with what he expected of me and I wasn't used to it, not that I didn't agree with what he was trying to do, but with the matter-of-factness of what he said.

Even though I thought he'd been a bit rough on me at first, I knew he would be a breath of fresh air; he brought some much-needed discipline to a dressing room that had lost it, following our relegation into Division Two. The impression I had at that time was that we had some big players on big contracts (for the time) not caring about themselves or the club. For me, that was disappointing because I wanted to play at the highest level with the best players around me.

Graham brought in his assistant manager, Steve Harrison, who was an excellent coach and the 'joker' of the pack and Bobby Downes. I'd only been in the senior squad a short time, and as a 19-year-old, I wanted to show him what I was all about. I was a shy, quiet lad who tended to keep myself to myself, but I soon saw something special in Graham that made me step up my game. I don't know what it was, but I liked him and I wanted to prove a point to him.

Some of the lads wondered what had hit them, from virtually a lack of discipline under the previous managers to extreme routine and order under Graham. For me, it was brilliant and just what was needed, but for some, it was a whole new ball game.

Clearly, Graham was there to sort out it out. He pulled no punches and was in no doubt the club needed restructuring from top to bottom. He was famously quoted as calling the team a "shambles" but it was his job to sort it out. Promotion was high on his priority list in the first season as well.

Of course, players talk and we all discussed what was said to us. I spoke to Garry Thompson (Tommo) and he was told he wouldn't be playing and that he "was a bit of a nightmare." Tommo was also told he'd be training with the kids if he didn't "toe the line." Tommo was told in no uncertain terms, that if a club came in for him, he was free to leave – he was seen as a "bad influence." However, he was given a lifeline by Graham in that if he changed his ways he'd be considered in the team. The writing was on the wall for Tommo from that day on.

Some players were told the gaffer wanted them to play a certain way so their immediate future was secure, but some, like Tommo's was less so. To be fair to Tommo, he got his head down and toed the line, so much so that he featured in every game from the middle of December onwards and scored 11 goals. In hindsight, it was just the kick up the backside Tommo needed to get his career moving forward. Even though they didn't see eye to eye, I think Tommo respected Graham.

I could tell that Graham was a true football man and he knew all about how footballers worked; when to give them a hug - and when to give them a rollocking. Around that time, I'd been feeling a bit lost and sorry for myself, and given the state of the senior dressing room, it wasn't the happiest place to be following our relegation in the previous season. I'd already had two different full-time managers and Graham was my third in 12 months – we needed someone to stabilise the team and I needed someone to help my game.

The rumour mill was working overtime before Graham took his first training session. We'd heard he was a stickler for training and apparently his players had to endure not one session, but three sessions per day. We soon found out that the routine would be as follows, five or six days a week:

8am: Morning session – running (it was horrendous)
11am: Football session
3pm: Tactics, set-pieces, strength work, for up to two hours.

I will always remember one of his first pre-season training sessions. We arrived at Sutton Park in two minibuses, one driven by our kitman, Jim Paul, and one by his assistant. Graham and his staff arrived by car. No sooner had we got off the bus, without any time to get our bearings or assess what we were about to do, Graham shouted, "let's go" and started running. We all thought this was just going to be a gentle warm-up run, getting ready for the dreaded 'death hill runs' rumour as it was known. Let me tell you, that unknown to us, even though he was in his 40s, Graham could run, and I mean seriously run because he had taken part in numerous marathons and cross-country runs over the years. As the pace picked up we all started giggling and taking the p*** thinking there was no way the gaffer was going to maintain this pace. But 30 minutes later the same pace continued as we strode around the beautiful scenery of Sutton Park. Half of the squad were floundering some 100 metres behind and a few of us literally just about hanging off Graham's coat tail! I could run back then, but even I was blowing. Then 45 minutes in I could hear Steve Harrison's voice encouraging the group that had tailed off to keep going and not get left behind.

It was quite clear 45 minutes into that run that the meticulous Graham Taylor had done his homework and knew the exact route he was taking as he had done a complete loop and it appeared that we were heading back to where we started by the minibuses. As we got to about 250 metres away I thought to myself, "I'm going to impress the gaffer here" and started to pick up the pace at the front; however, the quicker I went, he was equal to it. As we approached the minibuses we could see Jim Paul had set up a couple of tables filled with cups of ice-cold water from a huge Igloo cool box. I couldn't wait to get there as I was gasping! With 50 metres left, I was nearly there, then all of a sudden, without breaking stride Graham steered off to the left and up a dirt track. My heart sank, I felt like saying, "Gaffer, the end was just there in front of you!" Luckily I didn't have the energy (or balls) to say a word. You could hear the sighs of disappointment and disbelief from the lads behind as the water station may have just been a mirage in the desert. About 15 minutes later we eventually stopped. It wasn't good news though as we were at the bottom of 'Death Hill'. We rested for 10 minutes or so as Graham encouraged, or should I say, told us to keep going. We then completed, not one but ten 100 metre hill runs which had to be completed within 30 seconds. The journey back to Bodymoor Heath was probably the quietest bus journey I've ever done with my teammates. We then had to look forward to a two-hour football session in the afternoon.

Now, I have always loved running, and still do, but that

session was INSANE! I can tell you that first pre-season with Graham Taylor was the hardest I ever endured as a footballer. I must say looking back at that period, I was probably the strongest and fittest I have ever been in my life.

Thank God we only did those sessions for the first four weeks of pre-season. I recall another one of Graham's first pre-season training sessions at Bodymoor Heath, when the sun was blazing hot in the middle of summer. We all stood in a circle with Graham standing in the middle, discussing tactics, pointing at individuals, trying to get his point across. By this time the lads' concentration, including mine, had waned. Graham was shouting loudly at someone saying, "As for you!" It wasn't until the lads started looking in my direction that I looked up and to my astonishment I saw he was pointing at me, "As for you, I hear you're the wonder kid. I've been watching you for four or five days now but I don't see anything in you to suggest this. If you don't buck your ideas up, I'll send you packing to the Blues." I don't know what triggered him to say that about me – I hadn't done anything wrong as far as I was concerned. Maybe I thought I'd made it and it was only a formality he'd pick me in the first team – how wrong was I? At first I stood there staring into space, unbeknown to me that he was talking to me and about me, but someone nudged me.

For some reason, I really thought my days were numbered after that dressing down. However, I think he wanted to see some sort of reaction from me. In essence, he wanted to know if I had the character to prove to him what a talent I was. I think he knew I had the talent, it's just that he either didn't see it or saw something in me which needed a shove in the right direction and he could only find out by saying something like that. I guess I could have reacted one of two ways; I could have taken it personally and told him to stick it or react positively and prove to him I was worthy of keeping.

Luckily, I chose the second option.

I don't know what it was but something triggered in my head that I should start pulling my socks up and focusing on my game more. It seemed to change my whole perspective from that moment on; it must have been the kick up the 'arse' that I needed, because after that day, I got my head down and set about getting into the first team.

I didn't want to go to the Blues, that was for sure!

The nearer the season approached, the fewer runs we did and the more football was introduced into the training. At the time, we couldn't get our heads around it, why we needed to do so much running – we were footballers after all, not Olympic athletes. In hindsight, you can understand that by the way he wanted his teams to play, the high-press / high-intensity football, you needed the stamina to get through the 90 minutes. You had to be super-fit to play in Graham's teams. You talk about Pep Guardiola and his one-touch high-intensity football, but Graham wanted his teams to be high-intensity, but a bit more direct and never play long-ball; the ball wasn't just pinged in hopefully. Once that ball was played through the channel, invariably you'll get something out of it, whether it was a throw-in, corner, free-kick or a goal and you were guaranteed to be in control of the ball for the next four or five touches. The system was so effective at Villa because we had the players to do it. Subsequently, we had players like Gordon Cowans who would pick out those passes to perfection.

There was method to his madness though. Having spoken to Graham after I retired about his pre-season training sessions I discovered that not only was he conditioning his players for his system of play, but he told me that he wanted to find out which players were mentally strong enough to endure the training. That would have given him an idea who was up for the fight to bring Villa back into the big league.

Nowadays, every club takes nutrition and its impact on football performance very seriously. During my early years at Villa hydration and drinking fluids was not at the top of the agenda. During extremely hot conditions if the water ran out you'd have nothing. For hydration, we didn't have isotonic or electrolyte drinks which current players have now. Maybe we had Lucozade, but it was usually tap water. Some coaches weren't interested if you hadn't taken in any water, in fact, probably saw it as a sign of weakness if you did drink water. It was very tough, especially during the long summer days when it was baking hot; it was the toughest training I'd experienced.

Graham Taylor was most definitely a one-off. He was smart, genuine, personable, amenable and he was someone who you could speak to about anything - and I mean anything. He was actually interested in you as a person and if you had any personal issues going on in your life, he'd be the first to have a chat with you. If you ever needed picking up, he was there to pick up the pieces. He was a proper man-manager and a proper man's man; he was a genuinely good person, but above all, he was also a bloody good coach. I don't see how anyone can say a bad word about him, even though some players I know didn't take to him, but for me, he was brilliant, but I guess not all managers are every player's cup of tea - or vice versa.

However, Graham could also be a disciplinarian and would shout at you at the top of his voice if he didn't like something. I remember early on in his managership of Villa, he would try and get me to slow down and steady myself – I tended to run too fast and lose control of the ball and that led to some of my early displays being inconsistent. I knew this drove the manager mad; it drove my teammates mad and the fans too. As a forward player, the end product matters and early on, I wasn't producing it. What was letting me down was the ability to make that split-second decision, making the right pass or taking a shot at goal. It's OK beating three or four players, but if you shoot over the bar and high into the crowd, then that's not great. I have to thank Graham for adding some mental discipline to my game when he came in. He'd always do additional training with me and tell me, "Slow down, steady yourself, slow trigger" in training - wise words indeed. Once those words stuck in my head and with the additional extra hours on the training ground, I became a lot more consistent on the pitch.

Another example of Graham's disciplinarian side was at half-time during a game against Arsenal at home in December 1990. I strutted off the pitch, pleased as punch with my contribution. However, Graham had a different opinion of my performance. Once I'd got into the dressing room, he was reviewing the team performance, and when he got to me, he pointed and shouted, "And you, next time I see you on the far post, picking your nose, I'm f****** dragging you off – I mean it, literally I'm f****** dragging you off." It was the first time I'd experienced the wrath of Graham Taylor during a game, and probably not the last, but there was method in his madness because I came out second half with those words ringing in my ear and put on a man of the match display. I also never 'picked my nose' at the far post again!

The previous Villa manager had handed over an ill-disciplined bunch of players to Graham, but anything that he didn't like, he tried to change. One of the things he did was to find all the night clubs and wine bars that his players frequented and asked all the owners to inform him if his players were spotted there. I loved night clubs; even though I didn't drink, I loved the music and the atmosphere. I used to go out and enjoy it with the lads after home games, but after one episode, Graham took exception with some information he'd received about some of his players (well, one footballer in particular). He had a reputation of being a nice guy (which indeed he was), but he could tear a strip out of you, and on that occasion, he certainly didn't like the information he had received about me. Next morning, Graham asked me to come to his office, asked me to sit down and all of a sudden the silence was broken by a burst of anger, "Why the f*** did you go out last night, getting p***** and bringing those birds back home? If you want to be a footballer, you can't be doing this. You have to live and breathe football." When he'd finished his outburst, I had to try and plead my case; I reminded him that I didn't drink and assured him I didn't break any rules by going out with the lads. I think he knew I hadn't gone out drinking that night, but the association with the other lads was enough for him to give me a rollocking all the same.

There wasn't much that went on that Graham Taylor didn't know about, that was for sure, and that rollocking taught me a valuable lesson – not to go out with others when you're managed by Graham.

I certainly didn't do that again - at least I don't think I did!

There was a lot of good things I could say about Graham but probably the best thing about him was that he could get the best out of the players he had before him, no matter how good or bad they were. There were no world beaters in that team but he knew how to unlock the potential in everyone. Even if he berated me on the training pitch or in the dressing room, or he subbed me I understood very quickly he was doing it for my benefit. If I played poorly in the first-half, I could rely on Graham to tell me what I needed to do to improve in the second half – it was as simple as that. There was no second-guessing with Graham, you knew exactly where you stood. I quickly learnt to accept his feedback because it was always constructive, never personal, and for that I always had great respect for him.

While I'd always hear Graham shout advice out on the training field, you couldn't hear anything once you're on the pitch in front of a big crowd, but after a while, I didn't need to hear Graham because his words had stuck in my head and he can be attributed to enhancing my game in those early years. Graham was the right manager for me at that time; he'd worked with John Barnes and Nigel Callaghan at Watford, two great wide players themselves, so he knew what he was talking about. So, I listened – what more could a winger want?

Graham filled me with so much confidence before every training session and every game. When he talked to me before a game, he'd say something like, "Take the full-back on the outside, beat him; I don't care if you lose the ball, the advantage is yours, because you'll either get a free-kick, get a cross or shot in, or the ball will go out for a throw in. The only advantage to the other player will be if he got a tackle in and won the ball – everything is in your favour to take the defender on." Words like that meant a great deal to me as a youngster and I listened to every word he said to me.

Always after training I'd practice crossing from both the left and right side; I enjoyed playing on either wing but I'd put more practice in with my left foot. I'd always practiced ever since I was a little kid because it was the only way I would be able to perfect something. However, it was sometimes difficult to control the ball at times when I was running at 100 miles an hour. I owe Graham a lot because he spent a lot of time with me on the training field, practicing different things. Graham taught me the art of slowing my mind when I was crossing the ball while running at speed. It wasn't the case of slowing down my speed but training my mind to slow down my decision making. That was one part of my game I really wanted to adapt as I tended to run 50 yards down the wing, beat three or four players and fire the cross into row Z. After so many extra hours of practice it finally hit home and it improved my game no end.

Talking about moves during that season, I had the misfortune to get myself involved with an agent called Ian Glyn who promised me, a young, up-and-coming footballer, the world.

Well, maybe not the world but he promised me a better deal, a sponsored car, a boot deal, etc. It was Paul Elliott who put me in touch with Ian. He was Paul's agent and he had instigated his move from Luton to Villa. So, like a fool, I signed up with Ian for 12 months after meeting him. I obviously liked what he said and what he promised me. Well, why wouldn't I, as a 19-year-old, going on 20, being offered a new Audi, BMW or Merc? I'd not long passed my driving test so that was appealing. Comparing that to the company cars that the Villa players were driving around in, Austin Rover sponsored Villa at the time and most of the guys were driving Montegos or Allegros.

However, what happened after I signed with him was something pretty unforgivable. He actually went to the French club, Brest and tried to get them to sign me on a permanent deal. He went to France and represented me, struck a deal and took it back to Villa – all unbeknown to me. Given I'd just signed pro forms at Villa, I wasn't even looking to move anywhere. When Ian spoke to the Villa Secretary, Steve Stride, said that Brest were going to make an offer for me, but Steve turned it down flatly. With Steve there, the deal was never going to happen.

When Ian came back to me with Steve's reply, I told him that I didn't want a move and was disappointed that he tried to do a deal behind my back. After about four months I realised that this guy was a bit of a charlatan and decided I no longer wanted him representing me. I thought everything was OK and we had parted on good terms and walked away from the deal, even though I had broken the contract. I made it quite clear to Ian that I wasn't happy with him and he'd done nothing for me anyway. In hindsight, I was naive and was taken in by the offer and didn't read the small print.

In the meantime, Villa offered me a five-year contract when I turned 20 and I did it through the PFA who represented me, as I hadn't an agent – or thought I hadn't!

Two or three weeks after signing that new Villa deal, Ian got in touch with me saying he wanted his 10% for his part in the new Villa deal, even though he'd done nothing for me. He then told me he was going to take me to court for breach of contract. He wanted the 10%. I was advised to get the PFA involved, which was the last thing I wanted as I was really worried about it. However, the PFA spoke to him and threatened him with different things. One thing they found was the contract wasn't legally binding so they helped me get out of any deal with him and I didn't have to pay him anything. The whole ordeal took another two months before I was legally out of the contract.

Following that first bad experience with football agents, I had other agents start to sniff around me but I decided to stay with the PFA for the time-being. I must admit, the PFA represented me well and I was very grateful for their help.

***

Graham had a busy start to his Villa managerial career, signing a number of players during the transfer market – and getting rid of some of the players that he didn't think would hack it in Division Two. Some of the most notable incoming transfers were Kevin Gage from Wimbledon and Alan McInally from Celtic. My hero, Mark Walters left the club, so did Gary Shaw, Tony Dorigo, Steve Hunt and Paul Elliott, among others. You could say that during the course of the season, Graham had a wholesale clear-out of his playing squad

Formations weren't as important back then, not like they are today when everyone talks about their team playing this formation or that formation. It makes the game so much more complex, but back in the 80s most teams played a form of 4-4-2 and played a very similar way to each other. Graham liked to play a bit more football than his predecessors and it could be said he sometimes went to five at the back. Graham was often accused of playing 'long ball' but it wasn't.

***

I think it's time to talk about one of the most humble, likeable and funniest guys you'd ever want to meet. Paul Birch (Birchy), rest his soul, was a cheeky 'scallywag', and I say that in the nicest possible way. Not only was he a terrific player, a pleasure to play with on the pitch, but he was also a terrific person off it. Birchy was the life and soul of the team and always the one who got the brunt of the jokes. By looking at him and his stature, you wouldn't think he was the one who gave out the most stick to his team-mates.

Birchy was chirpy – always chirping at everyone in his cheeky way and always wanted to get on the ball. I'd say he'd easily fit into any modern Premier League side because of the way he played. Even though he wore the number seven shirt, he wasn't really competition for my position. On the ball, he was bright, sharp and busy. He wasn't really a wide player, more a central midfield general and didn't look to beat three or four players like I did. He wanted to move with the ball and get the team moving forward. Although he was a completely different player to me, I learned a lot in terms of both crossing the ball and his movement off the ball. Another thing I learned off him was the first-time pass, pass and move – something he was brilliant at.

One story about Birchy that springs to mind was when we had our six-week break between seasons. In those days, you literally did nothing for six weeks between seasons, then when the pre-season training started in early July, you had two weeks to get yourself in shape and prove your fitness. I can't remember what season it was, but on the first day of pre-season training I walked into Bodymoor Heath and literally walked straight past him. I looked back and still didn't recognise him. Birchy had bloated out during those six weeks and he was unrecognisable. He must have put on two stone in weight. However, within two weeks he was back to his old self. He was a hard worker anyway, but he must have worked especially hard during those first few weeks to shed those pounds. Of course, that would never happen these days as professional players have a specific off-season programme given by the club. They invariably have their own gyms and personal trainers too, so the off-season is spent keeping fit.

I think one of the reasons why Birchy put the weight one was because during the rigorous 10-month season we had to consume higher calories for energy and recovery. These additional calories were soon spent by training and games so putting on weight wasn't a major issue. Of course, during that six-week break, Birchy must have kept his same eating regime (plus a beer or four) but didn't burn off the calories because he didn't do any training.

Birchy was one of those lads who always wanted to be busy so most days after training he'd go down to the local snooker hall and spend a few hours playing the game he loved, something I never liked myself, but he loved playing it and spending hours passing the time. Having said that I did go to the snooker hall a few times to try and get into it but it wasn't for me.

On hearing the news of his illness and tragic passing at the age of 46, I was devastated to say the least, along with everyone else. I saw him three months prior to him finding out he had bone cancer, he looked fine but when I found out he had to have treatment and later died, it broke my heart. It was a tough time for me personally, seeing someone who had been with me for such a long time at Villa and Wolves, being so fit and healthy sadly passing so quickly. It really was cruel.

***

Life in Division Two was different for us. It took a while for our side to get used to the lower level of football as the first half-a-dozen results showed. The new season started poorly for me and for Villa. From memory, we only won one, drew two and lost three. A draw at Portman Road was followed by defeat against Birmingham City at home and then another defeat away to Hull. Things weren't going to plan.

I played in two of the first three games but I felt a pain in my groin area again during training after the Hull game. Although I managed to get through the pre-season, the season for me was something of a washout, in and out of the side from January onwards because of another pubis injury. For anyone who isn't familiar with the pubis, it's a bone in the pelvis area and the injury was caused by excess pressure put on it. In my case, the bones weren't lined up. In the past, I always had manipulation to keep the bones stable, but at that particular time I was really struggling, and at one stage it was so serious it was nearly career threating. I was in a hell of a lot of pain, constant pain in fact and manipulation alone wasn't a sustainable way of treatment. It used to take me half-an-hour to warm up before every training session or game, let alone try and get through the game. I would train OK then I'd find myself in crippling pain the very next day. I couldn't move and I was on a lot of pain-killers just to relieve the pain on a daily basis. It just wouldn't go away.

The only way of treating it was manipulation, lots of rest or as a last resort, an operation. In fact, Dave Norton picked up a similar injury that season which actually kept him out for the entire season, bar two games. Unlike myself, Dave had a major operation on his pubis. Just the thought of having that same operation as Dave put me off, given the complications that it may present years down the line. Although I grew out of it and the pain lessened the older I got, I had to continue taking pain killers and suppositories throughout my playing career just to keep the pain at bay. To be fair, Dave's injury was more severe than mine and the operation involved fusing the pelvic joints.

I saw a number of different specialists and one suggested I needed to have the same operation that Dave had had, but I didn't want to spend a long time out of the game just to recover from it, which is what Dave did. Even if I had the operation, there were no guarantees that it would be successful and I could get back to full fitness, just like any operation I guess.

In the end, what they did was give me anaesthetic so they could manipulate the bone in order to align the muscle by moving my legs around all over the place. Of course, while they were doing this I was fast asleep and had no idea what they were doing with my legs at the time. After a couple of months of rehab, I was still getting the pain, although it wasn't as bad and I managed to get back training. It was a scary time for me. My routine for the next three months or so was to train for a couple of days, making sure I had no symptoms but on occasion, I just couldn't get out of bed because I would be in so much agony. If anyone has had a hernia and knows the pain that causes, times it by 100. It was that painful. The painkillers helped but they had to. Although I didn't want the operation, it was heading that way, with the alternative of resting it for up to four months – with no football activity whatsoever. For someone who's conscious of staying active and fit, that was not a good situation to be in. I was told not to run but I could go on a bike.

The one thing that did help me was wearing the famous Vulkan shorts – a new invention in the late 1980s. They were a bit of a novelty at the time but they were used as support for groin injuries. They were the first Lycra-type shorts to be used in sports. However, these weren't for show, they were proven to help groin injuries. They don't compare to the light-weight shorts you get now – sportspeople could never wear them now because they were thick and would be too restrictive – they were as thick as a wetsuit! I became one of the first footballers to wear an under-garment under their shorts and I wore them during training and in games. To be fair, they helped me immensely.

After my lay-off, I came back fit, but not back to full-fitness or my best. However, it was great just to get back on the football field kicking a ball again. I did have a run of games from late January until early April. I came back in the away win at Maine Road in late January 1988, where I scored my first goal of the season. I seemed to like scoring against City, especially at Maine Road.

It was around that time that we signed David Platt (Platty) from Crewe for £200,000 in the February, which in those days was an awful lot of money for a player who was playing in Division Four. I seem to remember Graham was quoted as saying the fee was "over-the-top" because he had to increase the offer due to competition from Watford. I can't remember who it was but I got told by another player that Graham was going to sign an unknown kid called David Platt. With the departure of Gordon Cowans a few seasons previously, Platty seemed like a genuine replacement, even though we didn't know much about him. Platty was brought in as a box-to-box player, something we lacked, so from that respect he was just the player we needed. From Platty's debut against Plymouth at home, when he scored in a 5 – 2, win you could see he had everything. Not only was he mobile, getting into the right places at the right time, he was good on the ball, had great vision and a great pass on him. I can honestly say that he was the complete player, even at the level he'd played at for Crewe. As a 21-year-old he was mature enough to read the game well. I think his debut lit up the place and from that day on, he also lit up the training sessions with his enthusiasm, skill and maturity. He was different to anything else we had in the dressing room at the time, and he gave me something to aspire to.

David Platt was a guy I always liked to talk to. He was the epitome of a Graham Taylor signing. Even though he was a relatively unknown source, he came in with a big price tag so a lot was expected of him when he eventually signed during the season. I played in a couple of reserve games with him. At first he struggled - maybe he had to adapt to the higher league and the new surroundings and it took him a few weeks before he gained his place in the first team. I must admit that I didn't see his talent at first, but he soon developed and progressed once he broke into the first team. I think he had the number 11 shirt that season and on the odd occasion he wore the number eight shirt. He came into the dressing looking the part as well, smartly dressed and articulate and I think he was the example that Graham wanted to set in the dressing room. It was only when he made his debut in the first team that you could see he was class. You could see from his debut that he was a player who loved the big stage, and he got a buzz from that. On that day, he was on the big stage, playing for Villa, even though we were a team in the wrong league. I knew then that Platty would become a top-class player. He loved the limelight and he didn't mind the pressure; that pressure made him perform and that's a sign of someone who can handle anything. He certainly gave our team a lift.

The season ended better than it started for the team, if not for me. Although I didn't play in the last two games of that season, including the last game away to Swindon as I was an unused substitute, we confirmed our promotion back to Division One by finishing second in the league. In those days, there were no play-offs so the top three gained automatic promotion.

We avoided relegation from Division One and finished 17th in the following season (1988 – 1989). I scored my favourite goal at the Holte End in that year in a televised game at home to Everton. I had a feeling that I would play well in that game, even when I was warming up, I knew I'd score a goal. Alan McInally turned with the ball and managed to find a pass to Kevin Gage who played a perfectly waited pass out to Chris Price. Chris crossed a superb ball from the wide area into the box and it came to me at head height. I should have headed it but I decided to volley it and the ball flew past Neville Southall into the back of the net. I always remember that a week before that goal, I scored a similar one in training and the lads went absolutely berserk about it, saying, "Next time head it Dales." Scoring against Everton was like déjà vu.

That goal against Everton was probably one of the highlights of my season, although I did score another great goal in a 2 – 1 win at home to Luton, and again I scored in front of the Holte. I picked the ball up from a Gareth Williams pass on the half-way line, I took the ball past the defender, who was tugging at my shirt. As I ran away from him, he fell over because he couldn't keep up with me. I continued to run down the left, and after beating another two players, I dinked it over the 'keeper from a tight angle at the near post. I celebrated at the Holte End. I remember the Luton fans held up a huge banner which read: "STOP THE DALEY DELIVERY." I found that amusing, as they certainly did not! It was another amazing feeling, scoring in front of the Holte, even though there were only 15,000 in the ground.

Our Division One status was confirmed on Tuesday 23rd May when West Ham lost 5 - 1 away to Liverpool in their penultimate game of the season. I always recall Graham calling me at home some five minutes after the final whistle of that game and saying "well done" for the season and that the next (1989 - 1990) was going to be huge, both personally and for the club. I have no doubt that Graham made the same call to the whole squad, but his personal call resonated with me and I was going to do everything in my power to have the best season ever.

And so it proved, we did have a good season the following year. In fact, it was almost a great season.

If I thought the first two pre-seasons were tough under Graham, the training heading into the 1989 – 1990 season was even more so. However, unlike that first pre-season with the gaffer, we were hardened to it and more prepared. Even so, it was hard, let me tell you.

During that pre-season Graham set about the task of rebuilding the team, Martin Keown and Alan McInally left with defenders, Kent Nielsen and Paul McGrath, coming in. Graham was very clever in that he never signed any 'superstar' players but always bought players or picked players to fit into his team. At the start of the season, Graham signed two lads from the West Indies; one would become a superstar. Dwight Yorke (Yorkie) and Calvin Hutchinson were brought in on trial – Dwight subsequently signed a contract but Calvin was let go. The rest is history. We also spent £1.5m, a club-record fee on Tony Cascarino from Millwall.

When Dwight signed for Villa, Graham Taylor pulled me over and asked me to look out for him. He also asked me what I thought about Dwight initially staying at my parents. Dwight was then only 16, and, culturally, staying with a West Indian family would make him feel 'at home', with regards to food, upbringing, traditions, etc. I thought it was an excellent idea and ran it past my parents who were only too keen to help. Dwight, however, had other ideas. Although he was very respectful to my parents he did not enjoy staying there. My parents did everything meticulously and by the letter – a trait that I subsequently picked up as well. My parents cooked healthy West Indian food and really looked after him. Nevertheless, Dwight had to live not only by the rules of the football club but those of my parents too. In fairness to Yorkie, he came to England and wanted to be a success, which in his eyes was to adapt to English conditions and the way of life as quickly as possible.

He stayed at my parents' home for a few months before moving to other digs.

Dwight Yorke was a special talent. One of his first days at the Villa I always remember him saying to the lads, "I bet I can do 100 headers standing in this bin (swing bin)." The lads looked at him with disbelief. "Who was this geezer?" they'd say. Yorkie would then climb into the bin and start juggling the ball on his head. He did it with such ease, never once did he look like he was going to fail. In fact, he got to 95 before balancing the ball on his head and proceeded to manipulate the ball so that he could kiss it before balancing it on his head again. He did this a further four times until he reached 100. Everyone clapped and cheered, amazed at what they had seen.

He certainly was a showman. Welcome to the Villa, Dwight Yorke.

By then, I had established myself back in the Villa team and had played 25 games in Division One during the previous season. However, yet again we had a horrendous start to the campaign, winning only one of the first seven games. Graham was immediately under pressure. By the time we played Derby County on 30th September, the rumours were flying around about Graham getting sacked if we didn't beat the Rams. We won that game 1 – 0 with a goal from Platty after Dean Saunders missed two absolute sitters for Derby. We were shocking that day but we got the important result to give Graham a lifeline. That win helped us kick-on because we won the next five on the bounce after that Derby victory.

I think one of the most memorable games of that six-game run was the 6 – 2 home win against Everton, which was screened live on *The Big Match* on ITV. We were flying and playing some great football. Platty was scoring for fun and even I was getting on the score sheet. Things were clicking into place on the pitch, we were scoring goals and not leaking at the other end.

Another memorable goal for me was in the FA Cup Fifth Round away to West Bromwich Albion. There was a clearance by Gordon Cowans out of our own area and I ran on to the ball on the left near the half-way line, beat a couple of players, cut inside and buried it with my left foot. I seemed to score really good goals, not a lot of goals, but the ones I scored tended to be screamers and that continued throughout my career. I never tended to score tap-ins – that wasn't my game. Maybe that was the only regret in my career, not scoring enough simple goals.

That team were super-fit. I've already mentioned the way Graham liked his teams to play. The high-intensity football, sometimes direct and making use of us wingers. Graham effectively played three forwards in Ian Ormondroyd (Sticks) on the left, me on the right and Ian Olney or Tony Cascarino (Cas) in the middle. You could say it was a 4-3-3 system but whatever you call it, you had to be super fit to play in that side. Olney and Cas made runs all day long into the channel and I would sprint down the right-wing. By that time, Gordon Cowans had returned to the club from his spell in Italy. However, it wasn't all about attack because Graham wanted his players, including the attackers, to know their defensive duties. That part of the game was expected – you had to get back to help the defenders.

For me, there was a lot of competition for those forward positions, with Yorkie, Nigel Callaghan, Tony Cascarino, Ian Ormondroyd, Platty and Adrian Heath all vying for a starting place in that front three. I wasn't complaining because competition for places is good, as it keeps you on your toes.

So, what changed? Well, it was probably all about confidence after that Derby result. We had a very good team comraderie in terms of being a tight unit; we all got on really well and we all battled and fought for each other. We had a free spirit up-front, and they had a good understanding with each other, whether it was Sticks up-front or Cascarino. Sticks was six foot, six inches tall and stuck out like a beanpole, but he sometimes went out into a wide area, or he'd pick up a pin-point pass from Gordon Cowans down the middle. As with everything, it was all about confidence and kicking on from the bad start.

I'd had a full pre-season behind me, I was flying, feeling great and I kicked on from there. Like the team, I was playing with so much confidence, instilled into me by Graham, and I virtually made that number seven shirt my own. I was getting good reviews from the media and I was being tipped to play for England in the World Cup (1990). As a footballer, I can't tell you how much it boosts you being talked about in those terms. When you get 11 players who feel the same confidence and somehow 'click' you've got the makings of a successful team. It wasn't one or two players playing well and dragging us through games, it was the whole unit.

When you look at the defence in that 1989 – 1990 team, we had Kent Nielson (from Brondby) and Paul McGrath (from Manchester United), both signed in the summer of 1989. They were colossal for us. Kent Nielson was unbelievably fit – in fact he was a bit of a one-off. Not only was he super-fit, but he was also an absolute gentleman off the pitch.

I watched Kent training and something that was pretty foreign to us was stretching, whether it was pre-activation work before training or recovery stretches, post-match. I remember Kent going out onto the training ground before training had officially started (at 9am) and began doing stretches and getting ready for the proper training session (or before a game). By 9:30am he'd be in the gym doing more stretches and at 10am he went out onto the training ground, again to do even more stretches. However, while we were waiting for training to begin, we sat in the gym, either doing weights, chatting or having a cup of coffee and toast wondering what the heck he was doing and thinking he was mad. We couldn't understand why it took him so long to prepare for training.

The fact that Kent never got injured told me he obviously did something right and his routine worked. Watching Kent during that period made me first think about my own fitness and wondered if preparing before games and training would help my own fitness and help me to be a better player. The way I looked at it was, sure, I had the technical ability, but if I was quicker and stronger, especially as I was 8-stone wet through, it would help me immensely. Being so light, if someone blew on me I'd fall over – I was so lightweight back then. So, I can honestly say that Kent gave me the impetus to get fitter and get physically stronger. Not only that, but a key thing for me was also that I needed to become a more resilient player. I couldn't afford to pick up niggling injuries. Players like Gordon Cowans, for instance, could play with a slight muscle injury and it wouldn't affect his game because his style of play didn't rely on pace, whereas, if I picked up a slight hamstring I'd notice it and so would everyone in the stadium because it would affect my ability to run after the ball at pace.

One of the things that I worked on was injury prevention and how I could become more resilient from injuries. No player wants to pick up injuries, especially me, because my game was all about pace and skill. In those days, no one was really talking about sports science, but I started to become interested in new techniques by watching people like Kent in order for me to become a better player. I mean 'better' not just technically, but by being fitter, stronger and more agile.

After each game he would be the last one in, doing 15 or 20 minutes of warm-downs. We wondered what the hell he was doing, but he'd never had an injury in his life. It was normal on the continent back then, well, some of Europe anyway and they were, at that time, ahead of the game. We saw it as 'a bit strange' but we went along with it. Our warm-up during my early years as a Villa player consisted of an optional squad warm up or strolling onto the pitch minutes before kick-off, some basic stretching before whacking the ball as far as we could across the field.

I must point out that Graham Taylor was ahead of his time. One of the things he advocated was for his players to be fit and that meant doing lots of gym work. He was also an advocate of stretching and he'd often take sessions before a game. This was a time when we didn't have a fitness coach, so it was left to the manager or the assistants to organise the routines.

***

Platty was at the top of his game during the 1989 – 1990 season, and it was enough to get him into the England World Cup team. He was a perfectionist when it came to picking the right run;

however, he was a very clever player because he wouldn't do it all the time and defenders hated him for it because they didn't know what he'd do next. They must have thought that he made that same run all the time, but Platty would deceive them by not making it. He was a talented player. I remember him picking the ball up on the left-hand side, beating the defender, then coming back in and hitting the ball into the top corner, a manoeuvre that a typical winger would do. And what about that goal he scored against Belgium – who can forget that?

He was destined to be a top player and some player he turned into – and a lovely guy to boot.

I was also at the peak of my career and playing my best football during that same season; everything was going right, and it was all down to Graham Taylor being the Villa manager. However, throughout that season we were being told by the media that Bobby Robson's job as England manager was under threat and they were mentioning Graham as a possible successor if England failed in Italia '90.

In July 1990, Graham left us to become the manager of the England national team on the back of a tremendous spell at Villa Park. In a way, it was credit to him that the FA had considered Graham for the top job. He got us promoted back into Division One at the first opportunity and that must have gone a long way to add credit to his CV.

My initial reaction on hearing the news was one of sadness and shock. The announcement was made during the pre-season, so he had the chance to tell us face-to-face in the dressing room at Bodymoor Heath. That was a nice touch. He thanked us for all our hard work and wished us well. After the team announcement, I went into his office and wished him all the best. I'd just signed a five-year contract at the time and it included a bonus if I got called up into the England squad. I remember him saying to me, "Good job you signed that contract then!" From that I got the message that I would be in his plans for his England squad in the near future. While I was gutted that he was leaving Villa, it left me in no doubt that he would pick me in his England squad.

While I had been an un-used substitute twice under Bobby Robson, I desperately wanted to make a start for England and with Graham now the head coach of the national side, I was one step closer to making my dream come true. Obviously it wasn't a given and I'd still have to keep performing for Villa to be considered but Graham knew what I could do so that incentive was there for me.

On a personal front, Graham was the only manager I'd played under who really cared about trying to improve my game; he spent hours with me on the training ground and for that I was truly grateful. I credit Graham with improving my game 50% but hearing that he was going shook me a bit. Even though there were rumours about who would succeed him at Villa for a while leading up to his resignation, I felt an initial sense of loss.

Of course, the media were looking at the obvious candidates, including Gerry Francis, Arthur Cox and David Pleat, but Doug Ellis had other ideas.

Enter Dr Jozef Vengloš. The initial reaction from all the lads, including myself, was Dr Who? Nobody had heard of him when he became the club's first overseas manager on 21st July 1990. In fact, he was the first overseas football coach ever to take charge of any English club. We all thought Doug Ellis had lost the plot, but Dr Jo had pedigree, being manager of the Czechoslovakia national team before being whisked away by Doug.

It can be said that he was a manager ahead of his time. He was into football science, physical education and had a passion for football philosophy, all things unheard of in English football in 1990. This was way before Arsène Wenger transformed English football in the late 1990s.

Doug Ellis purred when he unveiled Dr Jo to the media, "He is simply the best. We have got the top man in Europe," he said, even though he wasn't a household name. When Doug asked the media, "Does anybody know who this is?" there was total silence from the reporters.

Were we ready for Dr Jo? Or was Dr Jo ready for us?

In terms of nutrition and football science, he was ahead of his time, even in Europe, let alone England. I remember soon after he arrived, the usual meal was steak and chips the night before a game but that went out of the window virtually overnight. I think British players were comfortable with the ways things were and always had been. That was the way Graham Taylor did it. So, when a new philosophy was introduced to us, some of the players resented it. Some of the older players struggled to adapt to being told what they could and couldn't eat and drink. I've said a few times before that there was a drinking culture at the club so that was one of the first things to change. Other clubs were still exactly the same and some of the senior players didn't see any reason why they should change their habits.

As a youngster, I had always looked to improve my game on and off the field; what could I do better to enhance my game?

Unfortunately for Dr Jo, he had a lot of obstacles in his way; although he had almost a full pre-season to change the players' habits and coach us his way, he was always going to find it a challenge. Everything about his regime was a change to the old guard. We had to get used to training at different times, different training methods and, of course, the food. Gone were the long runs up and down hills and maybe half an hour ball work during training. In came structured warm-ups which included stretching – proper pre- and post-match warm-ups. Dr Jo was anti-alcohol and believed in healthy eating, all the attributes that are common among every football club today.

To say that there was a lot of resistance from the players is an understatement, especially the older or more senior players. People don't like change for the sake of it – footballers are just the same. Thankfully, footballers today are used to very similar training methods because we have gone through wholesale change over the last 20 years and everyone is used to the modern methods, but back then the English game was 'old school' and not used to change. Having said that, I wanted to embrace the changes because it was a chance for me to improve even more of the facets of my game.

Dr Jo was hugely knowledgeable and intelligent. He introduced flexibility and functional strength work to our training regime. I've already mentioned Kent Nielsen and his structured stretching routine, but Dr Jo initiated that into the club, not only pre-match but post-match. Although Dr Jo wasn't everyone's cup-of-tea he introduced me to the world of 'Sports Science' for the first time, something that would play a major part in my life after my playing days.

Our diet changed as well, which was something that particularly interested me, even at that age. For instance, out went foods such as steak as a pre-match meal as its very difficult to digest and in came meals containing a good source of protein (e.g. chicken or salmon) and carbohydrates with a low to moderate glycaemic index (wholemeal pasta, baked potatoes). While the food changed slightly, it was more the time of day that we ate that changed. The introduction of eating wholemeal pasta and rice instead of its white variant was a big change for us, as well as drinking more water. Hydration was a big thing for Dr Jo and rightly so. We soon learned that drinking loads of water was like filling a car with petrol. An empty car wouldn't work properly, so the same could be said for a dehydrated body. It was essential for a footballer to perform for 90 minutes plus.

With regards to tactics, Venglos embraced his teams playing football. He liked the progressive approach which focused on passing the ball around before it reaches the forwards. It was a bit slower, a bit more European. For me personally, as a wide forward, I found myself doing less work. He wanted his forwards to be more intense and to remain up front and not track back as much, which was the opposite to what we were used to with Graham.

We started the season quite well, winning a couple and drawing one of our first five games. We then played Banik Ostrava in the UEFA Cup at Villa Park and beat them 3 – 1 before winning the away tie too. It was an important period of time for any English club because it was the first season back since the ban imposed after the Heysel disaster in 1985.

Then came Inter Milan.

The Second Round of the UEFA Cup drew us against the Italian giants and a home tie in the first leg. That Milan team, managed by Giovanni Trapattoni, fielded a star-studded team, that included Walter Zenga, Giuseppe Bergomi, Nicola Berti, Lothar Matthäus and Jürgen Klinsmann. We had two European Cup winners in Spinksy and Gordan Cowans (nicknamed Sid), as well as Platty, who had made an impression with the Italians only a few months previously in Italia '90 and was eyeing a move to Italy himself. Paul McGrath was missing for us, as he was suffering from a knee injury. Our team was inexperienced at that level, but we had defeated Banik Ostrava with ease in the previous round. We knew a big performance was required.

We were surprised by Inter and how they performed on that October night. They were poor and gave us loads of space; they gave me and Platty a lot of room to perform. I was up against their left-back, Andreas Brehme, who had scored Germany's winner in the 1990 World Cup Final. Well, I absolutely murdered him that night. Our defenders were brilliant and kept Matthäus and Klinsmann quiet all night. We scored first through Kent Nielsen, of all people, with a long-range shot from outside the box in the 14th minute. Mid-way through the second-half, Platty made it 2 – 0 when he converted a pass from Sid Cowans.

In hindsight, it was the best game I ever played in a Villa shirt and the game that probably got me selected for England. That game at Villa Park was watched by 36,491 fans and the atmosphere was electric. It was on live TV and guess who was co-commentating? Yes, Graham Taylor. Most pleasing of all, the Italian media singled me out as the most dangerous opponent and Graham was quoted as saying that I could become an England regular, just like Platty, with performances like that.

The media warned Inter that I needed to be stopped in the second leg. However, the return leg was probably one of the most disappointing nights in Villa's European history, as we were beaten 3 – 0 in front of 80,000 in the San Siro - Inter were brilliant. Giovanni Trapattoni, the Inter manager called it "one of the best matches of my career."

When you go into a second-leg tie 2 – 0 up, you think you're in with a chance, but that night was a nightmare. We were three down within an hour and I didn't get a kick. It couldn't have been any more of a contrast to the first-leg.

Fast-forward a few years to Arsène Wenger at Arsenal and the same thing happened. The Arsenal players who had done well under George Graham saw Wenger as a threat and at first didn't embrace the changes that Wenger was introducing. However, once they saw that the changes were producing results, everyone at the club embraced the Arsène Wenger way.

Unfortunately for the Villa team of 1991, change came a bit too early. Maybe Dr Jo didn't have enough time to fully integrate his methods. In hindsight, maybe Mr Ellis should have given him another season, but football is a results-based business and that 1990 – 1991 season just wasn't good enough. We just about survived again, finishing 17th in Division One. At the end of that season, he was relieved of his post after just one season.

Enter 'Big Ron.'

Celebrating my second birthday in style.

My beautiful parents, Pernell and Hezekiah.

I was the youngest of seven children.

Winning trophies at an early age - 1977. William Cowper School winners of the Handsworth Festival cup.

Always popping some style even as a child.

Just chilling with Pops.

My gear hasn't changed much since.

My last holiday with my parents to Jamaica before starting my journey as a YTS at Villa.

Pops may be having a kip as we watched the cricket, but he never missed a trick.

Happy times with Mom and my brother, David.

Holiday time with my beautiful children, Keiran and Sheridan.

My world.

An unbreakable bond with my children.

My debut season pen pic.

Young and with a fresh
curly perm - ready to take
on the football world.

Enjoying the open spaces at
the City Ground, Nottingham.

I learned very quickly
to ride tackles!

See ya! Leaving Arsenal's Nigel Winterburn in my wake,
before setting up our first goal for Alan McInally

In the heat of the battle football can still be light hearted. FA Cup Fourth Round v Liverpool.

This volley against Everton in 1988 is always talked about when I meet Villa fans and will always be very special to me.

Can't Stop the Daley Delivery – celebrating one of my favourite goals against Luton in 1990.

Bravery comes in many forms - I never shirked the challenge of taking the opposition on.

What a goal v Man City – from Sealey's kick, to flick on from Regis, to this volley the ball didn't touch the ground.

Wingers' union. Meeting Sir Stanley Matthews was a great honour

Nothing beats scoring the winning goal against Liverpool in 1992, in front of the Holte End.

Celebrating the winning goal against Liverpool.

Red Nose Day – Always happy times playing under Graham Taylor.

It was an honour to have played with Cyrille Regis (RIP), a role model on and off the pitch.

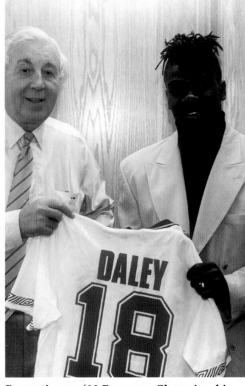

Presenting my '92 European Championship shirt to Villa chairman, Doug Ellis.

CHAPTER 4
Rollercoaster Ron

"What a character and what a manager."

EVERYONE KNEW Ron Atkinson, the former manager of Manchester United, was a big character. He couldn't have been anymore different than Dr Jo. Change was upon us at Villa and we were waiting for the rollercoaster ride.

During 1991, some of the lads who I'd played with under Graham Taylor and Dr Jo had left, including Platty, Cascarino, Sticks and Sid Cowans. In came Mark Bosnich, Steve Staunton, Dalian Atkinson, Ugo Ehiogu, Shaun Teale, Garry Parker, Earl Barrett, Cyrille Regis and Kevin Richardson. It was a completely new team.

It was also the last season of the old Division One (pre-Premier League). We finished 7th in the league, and I managed to play in 29 league games. Ron's magic was working.

The 1992 – 1993 season spelt the start of a brand-new era in English football with the introduction of the FA Premier League and a massive injection of cash from SKY. They had won the rights to screen live football to customers who had satellite dishes or cable TV. I was one of the 'new breed' of English players and at the peak of my career at the age of 25 so my name was put forward to SKY to represent the club in a promo advert to launch the football coverage for that season.

I had to go to the SKY studios in London where filming took place to shoot my part in the advert. When I got there I met up with all the other lads, one from every team in the new Premier League. The names I remember include: John Salako, Andy Richie, Andy

Sinton, Peter Beardsley, Tim Sherwood, John Wark, Vinny Jones and Lee Sharpe, plus others. Some of the lads had been there for a couple of days already but others, like me, were only required for the day. No one knew what to expect or what they wanted from us so we started to take the 'Mickey', thinking "What's all this razzamatazz about?" However, once we were told what to do we all got into it. My role was to be filmed doing bicep curls – topless! Back then, I wasn't muscular at all and in fact I got the p*** taken out of my pigeon chest – and still do to this day.

In hindsight, we didn't know how iconic that advert would become, even 30 years after the launch of football on SKY. It was great to have been involved in it.

***

The dressing room back in the early 1990s was a completely different place to what it is now – totally different in every way. We had some great characters in the Villa dressing room in those days; Nigel Spink, Dalian Atkinson; Mark Bosnich, Dean Saunders and Paul McGrath to name but a few. Throw the gaffer, Ron Atkinson, into that concoction and it would provide hours of banter, some of it funny, some of it not so funny.

Ron, just like Graham Taylor, was a one off, but that's where the comparison ended. Unlike Graham, Ron couldn't give a s*** about your personal life, as long as you did your job on the pitch. He was OK with whatever you did in your free time – to a certain extent, anyway.

There are so many stories about Ron, too many to mention in one book. Ron was a great character and there was never a dull moment with him around the place.

One of the most eye-opening episodes that I ever experienced was following a game against Derby at the old Baseball Ground, when some of the Derby fans tried to storm into our dressing room. A few of their fans managed to get in and must have been taken aback at the sight of Ron Atkinson having a physical fight with his namesake, Dalian! There'd been scenes like that before, during and after each and every game; players and manager would f- and-blind at each other in the dressing room, but once we all passed the white line and stepped onto the football field, all that had been said and done was forgotten. At the end of the day, we were all great mates who had one thing in mind – to win football matches.

We sensed there was division in the backroom team, with two strong characters in Ron and his assistant, ex-Villa striker, Andy Gray. It all came to light when we played Liverpool in the FA Cup quarter-final in March 1992, Ron's first season in charge. Ron and Andy had a massive argument, before the game, about who to start, either myself or Steve Froggatt (Froggy). Ideally, we both should have played, but Ron had his way and started me instead of Froggy. I remember Andy ripped into me at half-time about my lack of performance, which literally had me in tears, but I knew it wasn't personal as those things happen in the heat of battle. Somehow, we were level at half-time against one of the best teams in the country, but we were being battered and I just couldn't get the ball. I was eventually replaced by Froggy with 20 minutes to go in the second-half. It goes to show, as a winger, you're only as good as the service you get and if you're getting overrun by the opposition and you can't get the ball off them, who ends up looking like the worst players on the pitch? Yes, the wide men.

Froggy began his career as a youth player at Villa in 1989 and broke into the first team at a time when I had established myself as a 'senior' player under Ron. When I first met Froggy, he was a 14-year-old trainee and I immediately took him under my wing (so to speak) because I saw something in him reminiscent of me at that age. In fact, talking to Froggy about it years later, he wanted to be like me; he wanted to be the player that I was.

Only a few years later, Froggy broke into the Villa first team managed by Ron and we both played in his debut on Boxing Day 1991 against Arsenal at Highbury. We were good friends by then and never looked at each other as competition for each other's places. I've previously mentioned my ethos about football being a team game, rather than being played by a bunch of individuals and when Froggy made his debut, I saw it as a good thing for the team, rather than as a threat to my position.

I'm sure Froggy would agree, but he was a small fish in a big pond at Villa; a skinny kid who was playing in a team of seasoned internationals and being the youngest, he got hammered by the lads, but he took it all in and I think it made him a better individual in the end. Froggy didn't remember his debut for footballing reasons – he remembered it because of what the lads did to his new jacket and trousers after the game. He was an 18-year-old YTS (Youth Training Scheme) trainee earning £25 per week and only owned one pair of black trousers and a minging Tweed jacket which his father had bought him (his words, not mine). So, when he came in after the game, he discovered someone had cut the arms off his jacket and turned his trousers into a pair of shorts. He was devastated because we had a game on the following Tuesday and he couldn't afford to buy another set of clothes. Anyway, with no other alternative, Froggy got changed and walked home wearing those tattered clothes. The next morning, Froggy came into training and he noticed a new suit hanging up on his peg, so he asked Spinksy whose it was. "It's yours, son," he replied. We'd all had a whip round and bought Froggy a new suit. I think the lads saw something in Froggy that he was prepared to take the hammering, so they repaid him in kind. I think he learned a lesson and that was if you just take the hammering, you'll get respected by your elders. From that moment, Froggy became 'one of the boys'.

Considering what happened to Froggy after his debut, if that happened to a youth player making his debut nowadays, well, there'd be all hell to pay. You can't say 'boo to a goose' now and the kid would probably complain to the club. Maybe I'm being a bit unfair, maybe I'm not, but a lot of the modern-day players appear to be very sensitive to the type of extreme banter that we encountered back in the day. And I think that's a generalisation of today's society if I'm honest. You just wouldn't get away with saying some of the things we said in the dressing room nowadays because some people would literally end up in tears – and we'd end up in trouble. I'm not saying some of the banter was justified or the right thing to do, but it happened and it was a different era. Having said that, how we got away with half the things that we said and did back then, I just don't know. The banter was generally funny and never malicious. You could say it was a pressure release; there was a lot of pressure on footballers even then, but even more so now. A lot of fans would assume that we all had fantastic lives, even back in our day, but they don't realise we also got a lot of stick from fans and the media if we didn't perform and that created a pressure. All the fans want to see is the good side of being a footballer, but don't realise there are bad sides of being one too.

To be fair to Froggy, he had something else in his locker – he could play in more than one position. He was super-quick and he had the ability to adapt his game and play as a left-back as well as a left-winger. To demonstrate what I've said about Froggy, I remember a game that we both played in, against Swindon in February 1994. Froggy was playing left-back and I was on the left-wing. We went in at half-time goal-less and the gaffer (Ron) went absolutely berserk at us (which was nothing new). In the second-half, we both destroyed their defence, so much so that Froggy even scored from a diving header from my cross. Playing for Swindon on that day was Nicky Summerbee, who at the best of times was loud, argumentative and gobby, so we took it in turns to wind him up. We kept running past him and he didn't know which shirt number it was, let alone what day of the week it was. Nicky always had a nibble, but on that day, he didn't know which way to turn or what to say, because we were just flying past him.

We won the game 5 – 0.

The one thing we both found odd from that Swindon game was why Ron chopped and changed that side, after we'd played so well together. We hardly played in the same side after that game, maybe a few times more. It was a mystery to us why he changed that combination after we were so destructive in that second half and to this day, I find it difficult to understand why we didn't play together more often.

That Ron Atkinson team I played in was pretty unique, not just because it was a great side, but because of the number of black players - we had myself, Dwight Yorke, Dalian Atkinson, Earl Barrett, Paul McGrath, Cyrille Regis, Bryan Small and Ugo Ehiogu. I think we played an away game at Everton and fielded seven black players, if memory serves me right. Fair play to Ron for picking so many black players. 'Big' Ron was a bit of an enigma though back then. He was a 56-year-old man with 56-year-old views back in the 1990s and there were a few times that he'd make a comment to some of the black lads on the training field which just wouldn't be allowed in today's PC-mad world. In those days, saying something which would be deemed 'racist' now, was kind of accepted and it was seen more as banter than malicious racism. Conversely, Ron would take the p*** out of some of the white lads, too. Ron, to his defence, protected the black lads and stood up for them and allowed us to flourish.

I've met Ron since leaving Villa and I know that he was sorry for saying what he did about Marcel Desailly in 2004 while off air, during a match that he was commentating on for ITV. People make mistakes and he was very sincere about it. Clearly, Ron was wrong in what he said. However, having worked with him over a period of time, we all know he's not a racist, but some people, you may call them pundits, formed an opinion of Ron after that. Although everyone is entitled to their opinion, they haven't worked with him day in, day out. Every one of us says things 'off the record' in certain situations from time-to-time about whoever and whatever colour they are and Ron was no different.

One of the most memorable seasons I've had as a player was the 1993 – 1994 season, the season that we won the League Cup at Wembley against a very strong Manchester United side. However, it didn't start that well because I was in two minds whether to leave Villa or not when the season got underway. Italian club Udinese were urgently seeking reinforcements as they knuckled down for what was transpiring to be a difficult season in Serie A. I also seem to remember Spurs being interested in me at the time. The Zebrette (a delegation from Udinese) had apparently travelled to watch me play in October 1993 and were said to be close to meeting Villa's £2 million valuation for me. They saw me as an ideal creative outlet to play in front of Thomas Helveg on their right-hand side and as someone capable of providing a supply line for Marco Branca and Andrea Carnevale in attack.

When I found out about the Italian club's interest in me I was obviously interested and arranged to meet Gordon Cowans' agent, who at the time was Gianni Paladini, in one of his Birmingham restaurants. We spoke about the possibility of a move to Udinese and he asked if I'd be interested. The Italian League was the place to be then – it was massive. Platty and Gazza were already playing in Serie A at that time, so of course I was interested in joining them. I'd been at Villa about 10 years and it was at a time when I wanted to expand my horizons and to experience a new country. I'd already spoken to Sid about what Italian football was like as he'd done it a few years before (1985 – 1986). Having played Inter Milan twice in the UEFA Cup during that September and experienced it, I'm sure the Italian style of football would have suited me.

I thought it would be a good move for me. It's not as if I'd ever go to Birmingham City (not that I'd ever contemplate that anyway), but the move to Italy would have been something completely different.

The meeting went well and my mind was open to it.

Although Villa are my club, I didn't see myself playing for them for the rest of my career. I'd just come back from a serious knee injury and was getting back to full-fitness. We did well at the start of the season and had the UEFA Cup to look forward to. Udinese had approached Villa and a £2m offer had been accepted. That meant the club were willing to sell me. That told me a lot. I didn't want to stay at a club who were willing to sell me. If the club had offered me a new contract, I'd have signed it there and then – but they didn't. With the club still in the UEFA Cup after beating Slovan Bratislava over two legs they weren't prepared to release me. So, come the Second Round, against Spanish team Deportivo La Coruña, we drew the first leg away and in between the legs I'd already spoken to Udinese and had sorted out my accommodation, my salary, schooling for my children, cars, etc. – everything had been arranged for my move.

We played the home second leg and lost which meant that we'd been knocked out of the UEFA Cup. However, as with all transfers things change and suddenly, the permanent move was off and Udinese wanted to change it to a season-long loan with a view to a permanent move instead. Villa turned it down immediately and told the Italian club it was a permanent move or nothing.

I was gutted. Sadly, the move never materialised so I had no choice but to get my head down and carry on playing for Villa. I had decided to see the season out and see what happened.

As it turned out, Udinese succumbed to relegation at the end of the season. In contrast, we won the League Cup and I played a big part in that final so that was a great consolation.

I think that's what you call a 'let off'.

Then the semi-final against Tranmere should have been a formality, but football being football, it wasn't. We thought, unwisely, that we had a good draw and that we were going to Wembley even before a ball was kicked in the semi-final.

We got beaten 3 – 1 in the first leg at Prenton Park – and it could have been more. We were shocking. We never looked like the Premier League team – we looked more like a team who were below our hosts.

It gave us a mountain to climb back at our place in the second-leg. It put us in a situation that we shouldn't have been in. However, Dalian Atkinson's late goal in that first leg gave us a lifeline. It was a goal that I won't ever forget, because I found myself in the box and headed the ball into Dalian's path to slot it away. What I was doing in the box in the first place (and heading the ball as well) I just don't know. Once that goal went in I felt we had a great chance in the home leg. In hindsight, that goal saved our skins. It really was a get out of jail card.

We were still in the tie. Although we didn't need a team-talk, the instructions from the gaffer for the second leg were clear as daylight, "win at all cost." It was as simple as that. It was make or break for us. We had nothing else to look forward to as our league form was average so this was our last chance of silverware.

It would be a long 90 minutes, not only for the players but for the fans. We had to stay calm and stick to the game plan. We had far better players, attacking players who could hurt their defenders. For a player who was there on the day, on the pitch playing under that pressure, I must admit it was the best atmosphere I have ever encountered at a football ground. I remember when we came onto the pitch in front of the 40,539 fans hearing 'We Will Rock You' blasting out. It was an unbelievable atmosphere, electric and partisan. It was probably one of the most entertaining games of football ever played at Villa Park for a very long time; it will always be classed as a 'classic'. It had everything. It was dramatic and breath-taking.

Dean Saunders scored first and Shaun Teale made it 2 – 0 to level the aggregate score. Wembley was within our sights, but nothing was as straightforward as that because John Aldridge scored from a penalty to send shivers down our spines. We kept calm and didn't panic – as we were all through the game. Then I remember Bozzie nearly getting red carded before I crossed the ball to feed Dalian, who headed the goal to take the tie into extra-time. I think even before that, Dalian went on one of his mazy runs and nearly scored. That man was outstanding that day. Then, if that wasn't enough excitement for the fans, came the penalties. That penalty shoot-out was probably the most nerve-wrecking 15 minutes of my life. There was a lot of pressure on each and every penalty taker on both sides.

Penalties were tied at 4 - 4 and it went into sudden-death. Our skipper Kevin Richardson (Richo) stepped up to take his penalty and ballooned it over the bar. We were up against it now but it was Bozzie to the rescue as he kept us in the game and on course to Wembley.

I was next in line to take a penalty. I vividly remember walking slowly to the penalty area and placing the ball on the spot. I may have looked quite calm but I can assure that you my heart was racing and I was feeling the pressure! The silence was deafening as I stepped up to take it. Watching the game back, seeing Big Ron's face that he didn't fancy me scoring, yet alone the fans. The goal now looked like a five-a-side goal as I stepped up and calmly slotted the ball low into the right-hand-side netting. The relief of scoring was immense as this turned out to be the winning kick. However, Bozzie was the true hero as we emerged 5 – 4 winners by saving three spot kicks to send us through to Wembley.

Getting to Wembley wasn't easy. First we negotiated a tight two-leg, second-round tussle with our local rival, Birmingham City. Kevin Richardson and Dean Saunders scoring the goals in a pair of 1 - 0 wins. Next came an awkward trip to Sunderland. We were battered for the first 20 minutes and if it wasn't for Mark Bosnich (Bozzie) we could have been three or four down; he was unbelievable. We ended up beating them 4 – 1 but they created the most chances and were the better team on the night. Football doesn't lie; you need to put your chances away and on that night, we did.

The fourth round sent us to Highbury and, after Dalian Atkinson's goal earned another 1 - 0 win, then the fifth took us to Tottenham and White Hart Lane. A 2 - 1 victory there, secured by a goal from an unlikely source in Earl Barrett, sent us through to that semi-final tussle with a bang-in-form Tranmere.

Nothing is ever easy where Villa is concerned but we'd made it.

Who cared – we were going to Wembley to face Manchester United on March 27th.

There are many stories that I can tell about the 1994 League Cup Final. It was amazing.

However, our form two or three weeks before the final was

shocking; we'd lost three league games in a row and I had picked up a hamstring injury a couple of weeks prior to our game at Wembley so I was a doubt for the big day. It was a race against time for me to be fit for the final. I was getting treatment, morning, noon and night from our physio, Jim Walker. I knew full well that if I wasn't fit for the game against Oldham on the 19th March I wouldn't make the Wembley final eight days later. Jim told me that I'd have to have a full week of intense physio with him if I was going to be fit for the final, but that meant I'd have to miss the Oldham game. I didn't want to take the risk of not getting picked for the final if I hadn't proved my fitness, so I was desperate to get fit for the Oldham game. However, Jim went to see Big Ron about this and soon afterwards the gaffer pulled me into his office and told me to get fit and forget the Oldham game in order for me to be considered for the cup final. That news from Ron was pleasing and so reassuring. It gave me an extra week to be fully fit.

We lost to Oldham. We were shocking and I remember the gaffer tearing into the team after the game. It was clear that places were in jeopardy and changes were going to be made for the final. In a way, that was good for me personally and it changed my perspective. As we approached the final, I knew there were three or four training sessions in order to prove my fitness. I remember the training session on the Monday following the Oldham game. Big Ron pulled me into his office, prior to a big team meeting, to see how I was doing and reassured me again that I'd be considered if my hamstring was fine. While he didn't actually say I'd be playing against Manchester United, in typical Big Ron style he winked at me, virtually telling me in his own way I'd be playing at Wembley. It was the best news I've ever had. My confidence levels were sky-high and I was raring to go.

Ron was never a manager who would bring past performances into the team meetings, so during that Monday team meeting, Ron told us to forget our league form and to go out and enjoy the week and enjoy Wembley. That meeting made everyone relax and his words were a boost to the whole squad. The build-up started there, and in all fairness, from that moment on, our name was written on the cup.

There was no pressure on us as a team; we were the underdogs for sure, but we knew that our team could beat anyone on the day. It was a one-off game so we had no fear; we really believed in ourselves and believed we could win.

In fact, the biggest worry that I faced all that week was choosing an outfit for my then wife!

Ron broke the training sessions up during that week superbly. We even had a training session at the Cadbury World training facility; I think we played on their immaculate hockey pitches. We travelled down to London on the Thursday with our wives and girlfriends and stayed at the Royal Lancaster Hotel in Central London. On that night, we all went to an Italian restaurant and the players were told to take it easy and restrict alcohol intake to one or two beers – but it turned out to be a big, all-nighter p*** up and singalong. Everyone was, shall we say, a little worse for wear on the Friday morning, including Ron, so we didn't train properly at Bisham Abbey that morning. Ron then named the team and we just ended up doing walking set-pieces on the training pitch and then we all went back to the hotel. It was the most bizarre build-up to a cup final ever.

Can you imagine footballers these days doing that? Not a chance!

As massive a game as it was, Ron's approach to the build-up was to have us as relaxed as possible while keeping our focus on the game – and to focus on actually winning it. It was a difficult balancing act for a manager, but Ron was brilliant at it. It was never the case of thinking this was a free-hit and 'don't worry if you don't win,' but we knew there was less pressure on us than on United. We went into the game believing we could win.

Ron was used to winning cups prior to that final; he'd won three cups as a manager before the 1994 League Cup Final so the preparation was bread and butter to him.

Even on the day of the game we were all very relaxed. It was so relaxed that when I came down for breakfast, I remember seeing the Scouse comedian Stan Boardman sitting at the table with Ron. Big Ron had arranged for Stan to join us for the day. His job was to go round the tables speaking to the lads, cracking jokes and lightening the mood. He was very funny and Ron's idea of making the whole week relaxing and taking our minds off the final was pure gold.

As the kick-off approached, we all got on the coach for the

short journey to Wembley. This was a time when some players lose their nerve but Ron had a masterplan and that was to get Stan to come on the coach with us. I recall he sat at the front of the coach with the gaffer and as the coach set off, Stan picked up the microphone and started doing what he does best, cracking jokes and taking the Mickey out of everyone. The whole atmosphere on that coach was brilliant. Everyone was laughing, absolutely creasing! Of course, it was unusual and I guess people may have wondered 'is this the best way to prepare for a big football match?' But in hindsight, the answer to that was 'yes'. Stan certainly kept us all laid back on the journey to Wembley, that's for certain.

The way Ron approached the week with us was amazing; he just knew how to prepare a team for what was probably the biggest game in most of their careers. Having a well-known comedian cracking jokes may not be everyone's cup of tea, it certainly worked for us. That 20-minute drive to Wembley can sometimes seem like hours, but on that day, it flew by. Some players just stare out of the windows and over-think what is laying ahead of them, but on that short journey to Wembley everyone was focused on Stan Boardman.

How Ron set the team up was incredible and should be praised. Ron kept the team selection a secret but as it transpired he had a surprise plan – and it turned out to be a master plan. Apparently, he watched United draw 2 - 2 with Arsenal at Highbury the previous Tuesday, so he decided to deploy a five-man midfield, including 19-year-old Graham Fenton. Bringing in an extra midfielder in the unknown Graham Fenton was a stroke of genius. Graham had only played in five or so games for Villa and had only broken into the side in late February, so he wouldn't have been known to the United coaches or players. Ron picked me to play out on the left, Deano down the middle and Dalian on the right in a three-pronged attack. It was a typical counter-attacking line-up, with pace on the wings and through the middle.

United had Steve Bruce, Gary Pallister, Paul Ince, Roy Keane, Eric Cantona and Mark Hughes within their ranks – all top-class players. We were bobbing along in mid-table and had just lost at home to Oldham. United oozed class and confidence and were targeting an unprecedented domestic treble. United's form leading up to the final wasn't great, winning once in the previous five games and they had a once 15-point lead narrowed down to just three-points over Blackburn Rovers at the top of the league. They were still named hot favourites to beat us. However, form counted for nothing – it's what happens on the day that counts.

United were desperate to win the cup as much as we were, but on the day they just couldn't cope with us.

We were boosted before kick-off when Stevie Staunton was passed fit, despite not being 100 per cent due to a thigh strain, but he wouldn't have missed the final in a million years. Our back-line of Staunton, Teale and Macca looked composed and we were entirely comfortable and confident with the changed formation.

With 25 minutes gone on the clock that confidence was turned into belief that this was going to be our day, when Dalian stabbed home a free-kick from Richo and our fans erupted into celebration mode.

United's big guns floundered against our biting and snapping midfield and with 15 minutes left, the lone hero up front gave us some breathing space. Richo was again the supplier with a set-piece and this time Saunders netted. It was the breathing space that we needed. Funnily enough, at that time I felt we could win the game because until then, I felt stressed about us hanging on to the lead. However, towards the end Mark Hughes pounced from an Andrei Kanchelskis corner to bring it back to 2 – 1, leaving a nail-biting finale – probably about 10 minutes.

The pressure was definitely on United to push on for an equaliser. I think I'm right in saying Bozzie pulled off another world-class shot-stopping save; he was awesome that game yet again. Then, at 90 minutes, out of nothing, we broke their attack up and the ball fell to me from a Dalian Atkinson pass; I struck it with my left foot and it looked destined to go into the back of the net, only for Les Sealey to push the ball onto the post. When the ball rebounded off the post, it fell to Dalian to slot it in, but it was handled on the line by Andrei Kanchelskis, who was invariably sent-off. Deano stepped up to take the penalty and scored the winning goal. It was 3 – 1 and the celebrations began.

Those last few minutes went quickly, knowing there was no way back for United – it was just incredible; I can't describe the adrenaline and the feeling that we were going to win the League Cup Final at Wembley against one of the best teams in Europe.

Although nobody had given us a prayer before that game, we had complete faith in Ron's team selection and knew that we could give them a game on the day. We knew we were in with a chance, even if nobody else did. When the final whistle went, the relief was exhilarating; we were in Heaven. I was so tired, all I could think of doing was to lay on the ground, exhausted, but at the same time, incredibly proud and happy.

The strategy took United by surprise and the match was won and lost in midfield where our captain, Kevin Richardson, was voted man-of-the-match and Andy Townsend was, according to Ron's post-match interview – phenomenal. While we'd won the midfield battle emphatically there was another hero, Dean Saunders. He'd been left to forage on his own up front, but he still scored twice.

The League Cup might not be the most prestigious tournament in the football world, but this was one of our greatest performances for a very long time and one of Villa's greatest feats. Our side had to hit impressive heights even to get to Wembley after being allocated one of the toughest cup trails possible, including that mammoth semi-final double-header.

I won't lie, we partied hard that night in the hotel.

From the time I woke up in the hotel in London on the morning of the final until the early hours of the following morning I didn't go to sleep – it was a hell of a long day. From the final whistle until the very early hours, we were partying – it was fantastic! All the WAGs (Wives and Girlfriends) were with us at the hotel. I can't describe the atmosphere after winning that game. Even though I never touched a drop of alcohol – tell a lie, maybe a sip of Champagne – I felt as though I'd been drinking all night.

It was a night I will never forget.

***

The great thing about Ron was that he never over-analysed anything – and I mean anything. You couldn't compare Ron to the modern-day coach because he was so different, so individual. Ron's ideal team was mixing seniority with flair and pace. He wasn't a 'coach' as such – more a man manager, but all he wanted was for his team to entertain the fans. He'd very often tell his 'flair' players like myself or Froggy, "Go on son, entertain me." He had the upmost belief in his players that made him such a likable manager. As a player, you knew what your job was and you had the freedom to express yourself on the pitch. Wingers and 'flair' players are a dying breed – how many players do you see now skin the full-backs at pace and drill crosses in from the by-line? Not many, if any at all. Very often you have what they now call an 'inverted' winger, which means playing inside-out on the opposite flank (i.e., a right-footed player as a left inverted winger). They effectively become supporting strikers and primarily assume a role in the attack. Don't get me started on 'inverted' wingers!

Ironically, Ron was probably part of the reason why I left Villa in 1994, which sounds strange, but at the time I felt the need for a fresh challenge. Being a part of the club for over 9 years, I probably felt part of the furniture, maybe a bit complacent and that probably led to my demise as a Villa player. It's easy for a manager to toss you aside if you've been at a club for so long, but I felt I needed a change. Having said that, one of Ron's biggest weaknesses was dealing with contracts. Froggy told me he was negotiating a new contract with Ron at that time. He had played the two League games leading up to the 1994 League Cup Final against Manchester United, but he was left out of the final completely – he wasn't even on the bench. However, Froggy played in the League game against Everton on the following Tuesday night. That's pretty bizarre to me, but typical Ron.

Suffice to say, Froggy's Villa career didn't last much longer after that, either.

Looking back at that Ron Atkinson team, it's only now that I begin to realise how good it really was. One of the highlights, even though I didn't play because of injury, was that incredible (and ridiculous) Liverpool game at Villa Park in September 1992 when Ronnie Rosenthal hit the crossbar in front of the Holte End with a shot at an open goal. I remember Froggy and Steve Staunton literally falling over laughing their heads off on the pitch after he'd missed the open target. I think it was Dean Saunders' home debut and he scored a brace and quickly became a fans' favourite.

We won that game 4 – 2 and it started an incredible season where we finished second in the very first season of the Premier

League. It was an astonishing achievement; it was an outstanding team who played with flair and passion throughout that season. As well as being a great team, we had great individual players and no more individual than Dalian Atkinson, God rest his soul. I always spoke to Dalian in the morning before training on a one-to-one basis and he was quiet and reserved, good as gold, but as soon as the changing room filled up, he'd completely change into someone unrecognisable. He was a showman indeed and he needed an audience to perform, on or off the pitch. Off the field, he was shy but hilarious, probably the most insecure man in the universe, but on the pitch, he was something else. He was full of bravado, which was demonstrated by THAT goal at Wimbledon – who can forget it? I think it won Goal of the Season.

I first came across Dalian when we were selected for the England Under-20 squad. He was at Ipswich Town and had just broken into their first team. He was quick and strong and could strike a ball with both feet. The first time we played against each other was in a midweek League Cup game against Ipswich in 1988. Both of us were being talked about in glowing terms in the media at that time. We were both quick and on that night played against each other on the same side of the pitch, Dalian on the right side and me on the left. It became a personal battle of who was the quickest player; he would go bursting down the wing and I would track back and tackle or win the ball back off him. When I went on a run he would do the same, we both covered some ground that night as we both tried to prove a point. Let me tell you that I subsequently played with Dalian for four years at Villa and never saw him track back and close down as much as he did that night! We (Villa) won the game 6 - 2 but Dalian got on the scoresheet for Ipswich. After the game we shook hands and bantered about who was the quickest. We hit it off straight away and when Dalian joined Villa from Real Sociedad in 1991 we became good friends.

Dalian loved his cars and when he first joined Villa, he bought himself a brand-new Vauxhall Lotus Carlton, which was probably one of the fastest production cars on the road at the time. I remember having a lift in it along with two other lads after pre-season training session. We were heading down the A38 at speed and suddenly, Dalian noticed blue flashing lights in his rear-view mirror, so he pulled over. He was asked to step out of the car by the officer and give his name and address. The officer then told him that he was doing 110 mph in a 60-mph zone, so Dalian being Dalian, said in a serious tone, "110? 110? I was doing at least 135!" I think the police officer must have had his quota for the day or was a Villa fan as he let him off and told him not to do it again. When Dalian got back into the car he said, "Cheeky b****** said I was only doing 110, but I was doing at least 135." The guy was hilarious, a nightmare, but also a great player as well.

If you consider Dalian to be your 'typical' 1990s footballer, then I wasn't. For a start, I didn't drink much, I didn't smoke, and I loved my clothes. In those days, football was still seen as a 'macho' sport and most professional players didn't really care about how they looked or dressed, but I did and it didn't bother me what people thought of me. I wanted to wear what I wanted to wear, even though I knew I'd be slated by the lads in the dressing room.

I'd often turn up to training or a match wearing some outrageous clothes and some equally surprising hairdos. Luckily enough, I could get away with wearing such gear, unlike some of the other lads who just looked hilarious if they dressed up in way-out clothes. I wasn't going to dress down just because I was going to training; clothes were my passion – and things haven't really changed from that point of view today. Even though I dressed 'differently' to the other lads, I didn't spend crazy money on clothes. I'd live within my means and buy nice clothes which I could afford. Compared to today's multi-millionaire footballers, who spend lots and lots of money on designer clothes and flash, expensive cars because they can afford it and don't think anything of it. We couldn't afford to splash the cash in those days, even though we had enough money to live on and buy a few nice things with.

As a footballer, I was very sensible with my money – always have been, always will be. A lot of footballers in my era were paid a decent salary, especially in the Premier League era; but I bet a lot of them when they were in their early 20s didn't think too much about what they were going to do when the cash cow stopped, when they eventually came to the end of their career. Today's Premier League players probably don't have to worry about that because they are set for life, but we had to plan for our future at an early age – well I did anyway, and I think it made me a better human being by doing it.

*****

I think now is a good time to tell you about Paul McGrath!

There are so many stories about Macca, but I'll only share a couple. Everyone knows how good a player he was, about him not training and his issues with alcohol, but when he was sober, Macca was the nicest guy on earth. I've no idea how he could be p***** one day, then the next he'd play out of his skin for 90 minutes. He was a total freak of nature, but what a footballer.

We had a curfew of midnight whenever we went out as a group. One night everyone got back to the hotel on time, except one person. Guess who didn't return to the hotel! Macca had gone AWOL again and left us in the middle of some town. As soon as the management team found out, Big Ron and Jim Walker had to go out into the town with pictures of Macca to search for him. Finally, they found him drinking in a pub on his own. After trying to talk him into coming back to the hotel, Macca dug his heels in and refused to go back because he hadn't finished his drink. So, Jim and Ron had to sit down and wait for Paul to finish his drink before leaving with the big man.

It wouldn't surprise me if Macca is late for his own funeral. We played in a pre-season testimonial game in Macca's hometown in Ireland and he got smashed the night before the game. Nothing unusual about that but not only was he p*****, our physio, Jim Walker had to go out into the town to find Macca as he'd gone AWOL on the day of the game. After searching high and low, Jim managed to find Macca, get him sobered up and prepared for the game that afternoon. Jim wasn't sure if Macca was in a fit state to play but whatever state he was in, he'd have to play in his hometown as a huge crowd was expected to come and see him especially. On the day of the game Macca was still worse for wear and everyone knew he was, including Ron, who was managing the team. He knew he had to play. The team talk consisted of a few words from Ron, basically saying that he shouldn't get involved in anything. He was just there to make up the numbers and when the time was ready (15 - 20 minutes in), Ron told Macca he would get the nod and it would be time for him to come off. Ron told Macca when he gets the nod, he should pull his hamstring a bit and hobble off the pitch. Paul agreed and the game started.

Macca being the player he was got involved with everything from the first minute, to the disbelief of Ron, who couldn't watch. Macca went up to head the ball away but instead of making contact with it, the ball went flying over his head. Ron was furious and called for him to come off straight away. All the lads on the bench p***** themselves laughing and before Ron could drag him off, Macca went to take a free-kick and missed the ball completely. Ron ordered him off immediately. I think Macca lasted ten minutes of the game. When Macca walked off the pitch, he suddenly remembered he needed to feign injury and hobble off, so it looked as though he was injured. It was very amusing.

As a non-drinker, I used to watch all the shenanigans going on all around me, even though Froggy spent most of his Villa career trying to get me drunk by lacing my water with vodka, without success. In a dressing room full of some serious drinkers, I was usually the one who ended up being the taxi driver, too, but I loved it just the same.

***

It was around that time that I decided I wanted to leave Villa and felt as though I needed some help in getting a deal done with a number of clubs after me. I decided to find a football agent, so I signed up with Tony Stevens, the well-known and well-respected agent who went on to manage David Beckham in 2003. He was a 'Super-Agent' at the time. I didn't want an agent particularly, but I was advised by trusted friends and some experienced players to get one, given the amount of money that I was going for. Tony had a lot of experience dealing with high-profile players, including David Platt, so he seemed the right fit for me. I needed someone whom I could trust and Tony was the one for me.

It was probably a week before the final game of the 1993 – 1994 season that Big Ron pulled me over and said, "Look Dales, Wolves are interested in buying you – they've put a bid in. The club are happy with the bid and have accepted it. What are your thoughts?" I was coming towards the end of my contract at Villa but I wanted to make the right decision, so I asked Ron if I could go and speak to the Wolves manager at the time, Graham Taylor. I wanted to play in the brand-new Premier League but Wolves were in the second tier.

Wolves were going through a transition at that time, with the ground redevelopment complete and new ownership in Sir Jack Hayward. It was exciting times for Wolves, but they weren't in the Premier League. Molineux was one of the smartest grounds in Division One at the time – if not the best-looking ground. For me to drop a league the move would have to tick all the boxes.

So, I arranged to meet Graham at his house in Sutton Coldfield once the season had finished. My agent, Tony Stevens, accompanied me to his house, we sat down and talked from 12pm until 4pm about football and during this time we hadn't even spoken about any finances!

Graham had replaced Graham Turner in the March of 1994, with the club sitting mid-table of Division One, but he managed to secure Wolves an 8th place finish. In such a short time, he'd got the club moving up the league. We spent that first four hours talking about what he had planned for Wolves for the next season (1994 – 1995) and how I fitted into his plans (if I decided to join him), the type of players he was going to bring in and the style of football he wanted to play. He spoke about the club and what the new owners wanted for it. Graham saw Wolves as a 'Sleeping Giant' and wanted to make it one of the strongest clubs in the Midlands. The only negative was the training facilities at the time – they weren't great, but Graham wanted to put that right, too. All the talk of making Wolves a big club, those sorts of things needed to be done, so the one thing Graham wanted to do was to get the owners to invest in new training facilities.

We also spoke about Michelle, my wife at the time, and my kids, and what was happening in my life. He asked me where I saw myself, whether I wanted to stay at Villa for the rest of my career and about my future aspirations. As always, I was perfectly open and honest with him and said that if it was any other manager coming in for me, I wouldn't have been interested. The fact that I knew Graham well and what he was all about was a big incentive for me to meet him and listen to what he had to say. It didn't matter which club Graham was at, be it Wolves or Bradford City or whoever, I would have met him anywhere.

He made it clear that he saw me as playing a big part of his plans and that I would be his first signing.

Graham had done his time with England and had a break from football for several months so was refreshed and wanted a new challenge. He'd seen my own career progress, with both Villa and England, so he knew what he was getting from me. Like myself, Graham wanted to go back to the Premier League again and everything he said to me was in line with my own thinking and aspirations. He literally 'sold' Wolves to me.

We eventually talked about money, with Tony Stevens taking the lead on that so I went out of the room for half-an-hour while they thrashed out a financial package for me. I knew (and Tony knew) what I wanted, so once that had been agreed, Tony came outside and asked me to come back in. He then ran through the package and I agreed there and then. It was that simple.

The financial package that I agreed to was better than the contract I was on at Villa, which was amazing given that Wolves weren't the Premier League club. In fact, what I was going to be earning was significantly more than what I was on at Villa. However, due to my injury record, a lot of it was performance related, but even the basic was significantly substantial. I had no qualms in agreeing to that package and said, "Let's do this."

I will make one thing clear, and I'm being perfectly honest about this – it was never about the money. If I thought it wasn't the right move for ME, then I would have stayed at Villa. The financial side wasn't the most important thing for me; location and the manager had a lot to do with it. The other reason why I wanted the move was that Molineux was a place that I'd played at on many occasions when I was a kid playing in County games and I always did well there. Before I eventually put pen to paper I made a trip down to Molineux and visited the staff there and it brought back good memories of playing on that pitch as a youngster.

Leaving a club that I supported – and still support – and had been associated with for so many years was hard. It was a wrench to leave but the move felt right for me.

I realise that I haven't talked much about Doug Ellis – how can I not tell you a few stories about the great man himself?

Having been a youngster at the club and involved in the first team since the age of 16, I always saw Doug at the training ground looking to see what was going on. I seem to recall our first meeting when he asked my coach, "Ah, is this the young Mr Daley? The new talent." Doug had time to speak to everyone, even youngsters like me – he tried to make everyone feel a million dollars. After I signed my first contract he told me that I was one of the highest paid players in the club and told me not to let it go to my head. I say "highest paid" but we're talking £150 a week as a 17-year-old. As I've said before, that was massive money for me but I was hardly the best paid player in the club. He also said to me jokingly, "I hope you won't come to me next year demanding a massive contract."

Doug had a reputation for forgetting names, but he was brilliant with me and always remembered my family names and wanted to know how they were, Later in life, after I got married and had kids and even after I left Villa, he'd always ask about my family by name, although sometimes you had to prompt him a bit. I was always impressed with that side of him.

For me, Doug got a lot of stick from the fans, especially after breaking up the 1981 League Championship and 1982 European Cup winning teams, many of whom were still at Villa when I joined shortly after Tony Barton left the club in 1984. We could have gone on to do great things but it wasn't to be. It seemed he didn't want anything to do with that team at all. I don't think many Villa fans forgave him for that and I can see where they were coming from with that sentiment.

Everyone who knew Doug would say he loved to namedrop, and I recall one occasion when we were stopping at his villa in Spain at the end of a season. He showed us round the villa and would make a point of telling us about some famous painting and how much it was worth – but that's how he was and you either loved him or not.

Before I left the club, we embarked on a mini-tour of South Africa. Doug Ellis organised the tour but the real reason for it was to meet Nelson Mandela, who had been released from the Robben Island Prison in Cape Town about four years previously. Now, that would be a huge name to drop into subsequent conversations for Doug, wouldn't it? It was May 1994 and Mandela had just begun a five-year term as President of South Africa and we were there to play a match in the United Bank International Soccer Festival against Everton at Ellis Park in Johannesburg.

The day before, we were all invited to the Presidential Palace for a special 'shin-dig'. Mr Mandela wasn't there that day, but there were some important people and diplomats in attendance. However, we were told Mr Mandela would be attending the game at Ellis Park the next day.

Before that game, all the black lads in the Villa team, including me, were getting very excited about the prospect of meeting Nelson Mandela. I will always remember the day of the game, when we met Mr Mandela, how charismatic he was and how privileged I was to be in his presence, even for a brief minute, and shaking hands with him. There was a scramble amongst the players after he was introduced to us to get a picture with him or to shake his hand.

I have to say that meeting him was probably the greatest and most humbling moment of my life – it was a fantastic experience. I can namedrop to my heart's content because I met Nelson Mandela – not many people can say that. Even if it was only for a couple of minutes, I was in the presence of greatness. The guy just had a great aura about him that only a few people in the world have or have had.

Incidentally, Doug Ellis apparently turned to Mr Mandela and said, "Thank you for naming the Ellis Park Stadium after me." You can just imagine him saying that!

My only downside with Doug was that he didn't give me a testimonial. I spent nearly 10 years at Villa and as part of the deal that my agent, Tony Stevens, negotiated verbally for me going to Wolves, he agreed with Doug for me to come back and play a pre-season testimonial game. I categorically say here and now, Doug and Club Secretary, Steve Stride, agreed to it just before I left Villa. Obviously, there was an association with Graham Taylor and it was agreed a game against Wolves would be ideal. However, for over a year nothing happened, nothing had been discussed, so I asked Doug if we could get the game organised and his comment to me was, "What game?" I reminded him of the verbal agreement and that we shook hands on it, but he denied any recollection of it and even went as far as saying, "You only did nine-and three-quarter years." I really wanted a testimonial game, but it was that evident the club didn't. That went on for months and the longer it went on, the less chance I had of getting one arranged. To clarify things, I went back to

Graham Taylor and told him this but there was nothing he could do. I was quite annoyed and upset with Doug, but he was fairly stubborn in his stance. I wasn't bitter but I was disappointed. In hindsight, I should have had it written into my contract, but I didn't and that was my fault.

I don't think I have ever told that story before because I didn't want it to be made public that I was disappointed in Doug.

It was time to move on!

All good things have to come to an end and my nine-year Villa career ended after 233 first team appearances and 31 goals. I'd also been capped seven times for England. I'd had some good times at Villa, most notably the League Cup win, and nearly winning the league in the 1989 – 1990 season under Graham Taylor and the 1992 – 1993 season under Ron Atkinson.

At the age of 26, I was about to embark on a new chapter of my career, away from Villa Park.

CHAPTER 5
Life After Villa

"It was a wrench moving from Villa."

GRAHAM TAYLOR returned to club management in March 1994 with Wolverhampton Wanderers, after his spell with the England national team, and made Froggy and myself two of his first signings in the summer of that year.

I joined on 30th June 1994, for a (then) club record of £1.25m on a four-year contract and joined the squad for the 1994 – 1995 Division One campaign (second tier). However, something that wasn't known at the time, and hasn't been divulged before, is that my medical wasn't straight forward. The doctor told Graham that there was a problem with my knee and he wanted to investigate it before I signed, but Graham said "No, I'm happy with it – we're going ahead with it!" I think Graham knew that if the doctor had insisted on looking into the issue, then I would have failed the medical and I wouldn't have signed for Wolves.

More to the point, the one thing that it did show was that Graham was desperate to get me into the club. He knew what I could do and I wanted to play for Graham – it was as simple as that. If that combination wasn't there and there was any other manager at Wolves, that investigation would have taken place. In hindsight, my subsequent career would have looked different – it may have jeopardised my football career there and then. It would have meant, at least, having yet another operation – and I'd have remained at Villa.

The issue that the doctor had found stemmed from the cruciate injury I'd had 18 months previously. I came back from that, no problem, but I played in an end of season friendly for Villa against West Bromwich Albion, it could have been a testimonial or something, and I picked up a knee injury during that game. It didn't seem too serious and I played the game out as it didn't really give me any problems and it had cleared up within a fortnight. So, I signed my Wolves contract without the medical being passed. It was a major risk for the club, but Graham wanted to get the deal done. I subsequently found out that the doctor who found the issue on the X-Ray resigned because of it.

There were some familiar names already in the squad like Gordon Cowans and Paul Birch, who we knew at Villa, together with seasoned pros like Steve Bull. There were some other big characters in that dressing room as well as Bully, having Don Goodman come in from Sunderland for over a £1m. Throw into the mix: Mark Venus, Dean Richards, Geoff Thomas, and Neil Emblen, Graham eventually spent over £4.5m – massive money for a second-tier club in those days. We had some strong characters in the dressing room, so you can imagine that it was going to be a rollercoaster season, on and off the pitch. It was already an all-star cast.

Wolves were a huge club and were desperate to get into the Premier League; Graham was given £5m to spend on player recruitment that season and he sold the 'ambition' of Wolves to me, and subsequently, to Froggy.

If I remember rightly, one of the first things that I did at Wolves was to meet The Queen, shortly after meeting another great person in Nelson Mandela only a month or so before. The Queen visited Molineux and Paul Birch and I were introduced to Her Majesty. I can't remember what the occasion was though and to be honest, I can't remember what she said to me apart from shaking my hand and asking if I was OK. It was a very brief encounter but still an amazing honour, but there was no full-blown conversation about me being Wolves' record signing.

At the time that I signed, the club was owned by Sir Jack Hayward. He loved that club with a passion – perhaps too much. He had so much involvement in the club that some of his decisions were probably from the heart rather than from the head, but I always got on with him and he was a lovely guy to speak to. I had the upmost respect for him.

The first few weeks at Wolves were a bit awkward. The Wolves legend, Steve Bull, a big character in the dressing room, didn't speak to me (or to Froggy) for the first couple of weeks. He was a bit offish with us, probably because he saw two big signings from the Premier League come into the dressing room thinking that they were the bees' knees. Not only that, but we also both couldn't understand a word he was saying and I think we both spent most of that time just nodding at him! Having said that, Bully soon warmed to us and turned out to be a great guy and eventually became a really good friend. And we started to understand his strong Black Country accent a bit!

There was lots of banter in that dressing room – all of it was just good-natured and never nasty. However, one day, imagine my horror when I realised that what had started out as a bit of fun, was going to have a long-term effect on my hair.

During my injury plagued career at Wolves, banter was the go-to to help me mentally through it. I'll always remember halfway through my playing career at Wolves I was joined by a long list of other players with long term injuries, Steve Froggatt, Steve Bull, Geoff Thomas, John De Wolf. We would play lots of practical jokes which included cutting players' socks, defacing disapproved items of clothing, or leaving milk hidden in players cars. The list could go on. One day one practical joker decided to put hair removing cream in my hat. I didn't have a clue and nobody decided to tell me at the time. I was in a panic when within a few days I noticed patches in my hair and a couple of my locks were hanging by a thread. I did not find this funny AT ALL! As a result I decided to shave it all off but kept a small ponytail for my infamous 'Yul Brynner' haircut.

Talking about hair styles, even as a young child my appearance was very important to me. I took pride in what I wore and even more so my hair. During my time at Villa, I had an array of haircuts that are still talked about today. At no time did I have a hair style just for shock or wow value, it was just a way of expressing myself. It was my hairdresser, Lurline, who inspired my haircuts. We would discuss what I would like then she put her own little spin on it. I was always satisfied with the results. To be honest I wasn't really bothered what the fans and press thought about my hair or the way I dressed – it was like water off a duck's back to me, To this day though, I hear many a story from Villa fans who grew up watching me going to their hairdressers and, to their bemusement, asking for a 'Tony Daley' haircut. My teammates used to take the p*** something rotten but I didn't bat an eyelid. I felt that this was a good thing as in the end they just accepted it because I didn't bite. I truly did it for myself.

***

At the start of that first season, I was raring to go with my new club. I was looking forward to playing with Froggy; both of us on the wings, and with Bully and Goodman in the centre, we should have been a frightening combination. I was relishing playing in Division One because the level wasn't the same as the Premier League, so it should have been easier for players like us to adapt. I was 26-years old when I went to Wolves, in the prime of my career and fitter than I'd ever been – I was flying in pre-season. I was relishing the challenge of what should have been the best part of my career. I honestly felt better in terms of my pace and playing ability than I did at any stage of my Villa career.

I do remember scoring a (rare) header in pre-season, courtesy of a super cross by Froggy, but that was the only highlight because that first season turned out to be a disaster for me. My first season at Wolves ended suddenly, as quickly as it had begun because I tore my cruciate ligament during a friendly game. This was after training for two weeks and scoring a couple of goals in the first couple of games. In fact, during a training session early on in the tour, I went to retrieve the ball and my knee went, but after a while it had settled down again.

When I got taken off for the friendly game in Sweden, the physios reckoned I'd unknowingly done my cruciate then. They reckoned the injury stemmed from that friendly game against West Brom when I was at Villa. I had to leave the tour early and went back to England to see a surgeon and have some tests. The tests revealed that I'd probably had the injury for six months; I'd been playing with a cruciate ligament injury for half a season! The surgeon didn't want to do an operation at first and suggested that the injury could be managed by having three months of conservative treatment, which meant building muscle and looking after the knee from the end of July until October. During that time, I had no problems at all and built some muscle back around the knee. I started training with the first team at the start of October and felt great and then was picked as a substitute for the home game against Millwall. With 20 minutes to go, I was asked to warm-up and then Graham asked me to get on the pitch. The reception I got from the Wolves fans when I took to the pitch for the first time in a Wolves shirt was fantastic – it was unbelievable really. I'd been on the pitch for 90 seconds and I went into a challenge with Ben Thatcher, who cut inside me as I went to turn to track him. It was at that point that my knee went. I hadn't even kicked a ball in the famous gold and black. I tried to hobble on but had to stop and went down in a heap. The physio came on and I told him it had settled down a bit and said I wasn't coming off – not a cat in hell's chance. I quickly got up and told the physio (nicely) to clear off but as I took a few more steps I felt it go again and collapsed in a heap on the ground in agony. I'd been on the pitch for literally eight minutes but spent six of those minutes on the ground. Of course, this time I didn't dispute the physio's advice and came off the pitch.

I felt like the world had collapsed on me. As a footballer, there's nothing worse than coming back from a serious injury, only for it to re-appear in your comeback game. For me, it felt like it had come out of the blue; I'd been training for a couple of weeks with no reoccurrence of the swelling, the rehab had gone well and I was fit enough to play. It was so hard to take in.

A couple of days after that Millwall game I went to see the surgeon again and he suggested that I have an operation to have a cruciate ligament reconstruction.

I was out for nine months after the operation.

It was one of the lowest periods of my football career. I was facing nine months out of the game and I'd only played 90 seconds of football for Graham Taylor and Wolves.

It was a rollercoaster season for Graham and for Wolves. In my absence, we had scored 77 goals, more than any other team in the league and 10 more than champions Middlesbrough, but we had conceded 61 goals. Notts County, who were relegated, had conceded 66. We had quite a squad to choose from as well, with Bully, David Kelly, Froggy, Geoff Thomas, Gordon Cowans, Mark

Venus, Dean Richards, John de Wolf, Neil Emblen, Don Goodman, Mark Rankine, Robbie Dennison and Andy Thompson. Another player who was brought in was Mark Walters, one of my heroes at Villa, even though he's only a few years older than me. Wally was brought in on loan from Liverpool. It was a total surprise to everyone, including myself. Being a wide player, he was brought in as cover for myself and Froggy.

There were some big names in that dressing room, that's for sure. Expectations for that season were huge but we had a leaky defence, a prolific attack and a gung-ho approach to every game. That cocktail spelt disaster. However, the entertainment was never in short supply and the stadium was packed week in, week out – we were the equivalent of Kevin Keegan's Newcastle United team.

Wolves made the play-offs by finishing fourth during that 1994 – 1995 season and that's another campaign I missed out on.

The 1995 – 1996 season was probably my most efficient season of my Wolves career as I played 16 league games, scoring three goals. The one I'm most proud of and remember the most was a screamer I scored against Watford at Vicarage Road in a 1 – 1 draw. I picked the ball up at the corner of the box, played it to Gordon Cowans, who played it back to me and from about 25 yards I let loose with my left foot from outside the box and it flew into the top corner.

During November and December 1995, I was approached to take part in a TV documentary called '*Respect*', which featured some of the biggest names in British sport. It was produced in Birmingham by Central TV and was a series of half-hour, 'fly-on-the-wall' programmes which focused on Afro-Caribbean sportspeople who have gained 'respect' through their single-minded determination to their chosen sport. Alongside me, were Gladstone Small (cricket), John Regis (athletics), Lennox Lewis (boxing) and Martin Offiah (Rugby Union) and it was presented by Garth Crooks.

It was not a set-up and they didn't try and catch me out with their questioning – it was done very professionally. It was meant to give the viewers a snippet of my life, behind the scenes – something that people didn't have access to in those days, not as much as they do today. The film crew came into my house for three days and talked about my life, my family and only touched on the football side – it wasn't a football documentary, more to do with how I lived my life as a (black) footballer. They particularly featured on my lifestyle, the way I dressed and went about things. Of course, we did talk about football – the advantages and disadvantages of being a footballer and what it gives you. The show was ahead of its time as that kind of programme hadn't been done before. I didn't really want to do it at first as I was really shy, but I really enjoyed it, even though it was a 'no holds barred' kind of documentary. In fact, I heard subsequently that the episode that I was featured in was the most watched of the six shows they filmed.

Coincidentally, I ruptured my patella tendon during the following pre-season in Germany, so that season was a write-off too. I was devastated. How can someone have so much bad luck with so many horrific injuries in such a short time? You can live with minor injuries like calf strains etc., but these were major injuries and potentially career threatening ones too. Those injuries happened during what should have been the best part of my career. It was not only physically draining, having those bad injuries, but it was mentally tough too. I don't think fans realise what a strain it is for a football player (or any sportsman) being out injured and not being able to contribute to the team.

I wasn't in a good place and I didn't see anything changing. Those were dark days, and especially hard on matchdays when the lads were on the pitch performing, but I was either on the treatment table or watching in the stands and it affected me big time. Even though I was miserable inside, I'd never let it show and would always have a smile on my face. Looking back, that's one thing that I've changed about myself – being able to show my true feelings and not mask them like I used to. Maybe the mask I had at Wolves, being on the treatment table more than I liked, was the one thing I regretted from my playing career. Inside I was deeply depressed and unhappy, not being able to play week in, week out and I was having problems off the pitch as well. It got so bad that I had IBS (Irritable Bowel Syndrome) and that led me to have even more time off. However, only the club doctor knew about it at the time. It was the worse period of my life and I wasn't happy with my life. I'd never had IBS before and I was told that it was the outcome from the stress of being injured and not being able to cope with not playing. I was having numerous stomach pains and convulsions on a daily basis so I went to see a consultant about it.

The prognosis was basically to have less stress in my life.

I ended up having the IBS for about eight or nine months or maybe more – it was awful. I can't describe the agony I was in every single day – it was a real dark time for me. Having said that, I don't think I could have got through that period without the love of my kids and the solace of the gym, lifting weights to try and relieve some of the stress and tension inside me. The time that I spent in the gym helped me to focus on trying to get back to fitness and back on the park.

I was worried about my career because some of the injuries I had were serious and career-threatening and I didn't know what I'd do if I was told I couldn't play again. Doctors apart, I don't think anybody knew what I was going through and that wasn't healthy. If I was facing that situation now, I'd have all the help in the world and it wouldn't be an issue, but back then, mental health issues were just not talked about.

The dressing room wasn't an environment (in those days) where you'd openly admit that you were having a hard time and you needed some help – it just wasn't done. In the 1980s and 1990s, it wasn't 'macho' to speak out about your own emotions – it wasn't the done thing back then; it probably still isn't to a certain extent, but that's how it was, rightly or wrongly. Personally, I found it difficult to speak out and maybe that's why I hid it for so long. The IBS lasted about eight or nine months and eventually, I did seek help; Graham Taylor was really good to talk to and it was a massive help to get my issues out into the open.

That's one of the more positive things that has happened in the game that has improved; the help that is provided for players now is a complete contrast to those days. Footballers talking about mental health is an everyday occurrence and there's so much publicity about it and so much help available that there's no excuse for players to suffer anymore; players don't have to keep quiet about their issues, like we used to do. Although there has been an improvement in footballers opening up about their issues, the fear of being dropped if they do still looms large. There have been a number of well-publicised cases in the last 10 years, which has helped to bring the subject to the fore, but there is still a lot more that could be done. We never, ever talked about the way we were feeling, it just wasn't the done thing. It would have been seen as a sign of weakness, and I think there is still that fear-factor, even in today's game, which is a shame, but on the whole, things are a lot better.

That's the one good thing that's changed in the game nowadays and long may it continue.

There was high expectation put upon me following my signing for Wolves; the pressure of me being brought in to help the club's promotion chase was immense and I wanted to establish myself in the side quickly, but unfortunately I found myself injured most of the time, but that pressure never went away. However, even when the injury healed, the pressure and stress didn't relent. There was a different type of pressure, the pressure of returning to fitness and playing again and that hit the mental side of my game as well.

I have spoken about my first game back from injury, when I came on as a substitute against Millwall at home, and there was a big build up and expectation for my return. The media made a big thing of my comeback and the pressure was on me again. It was around this time that I went to see the famous spiritualist and heeler, Eileen Drewery. I think that it was in sometime in 1997 when I was invited to Eileen's house in Reading, as I'd been in touch with her and was interested in what she could do for me. The physio at Wolves at the time was Dave Hancock, and although he was doing a great job, I wanted to try an alternative therapy to try and heel my injury quicker. Dave was OK with me going to seek alternative help and I went ahead and spoke to Eileen and decided to go and see her.

So, I turned up at Eileen's house and was greeted by her and her husband, and lo and behold, Glenn Hoddle was there too. Glenn was the England manager at the time, so seeing him there was a nice surprise, although I didn't know Glenn that well.

After a brief chit-chat with Glenn, I made my way to Eileen's consulting room. Eileen and I sat in the room and I told her what my injury was and what treatment I was having and then she explained what the process would be, which basically consisted of her putting her hand on the part of my body (my knee) that I was having trouble with. Now, I wasn't into spiritualism or alternative therapy at the time so I went there with an open mind and a bit of apprehension.

Once I'd relaxed Eileen rested her hand on my injured knee and after a few minutes I could feel the heat that it had generated. Eileen said the amount of heat generated was unbelievable. My scepticism vanished and I began to think there's definitely something in it. Eileen then said, "you've got a massive aura around you," which meant I had a lot of protection around me and especially around my knee. She went on to say that I had a 'guardian' around me, protecting me, creating the heat. Not only that, but she started describing my Grandma as my 'guardian'. When Eileen was describing my Grandma, given that she'd never met her and I'd given her no clues whatsoever, I felt a chill go up my spine. She sensed my Grandma was all around me, protecting me everywhere I went.

While I was there, she read my palm and told me about some things that would happen in the near future. Looking back, some of the things that she described actually happened, although she didn't go into any sort of detail, some of her predictions were spot on. What was amazing about it was that none of it was guesswork. She wasn't fishing for information or anything like that, but what she came out with was very specific and very near to the point. She was giving me specific future dates and dates of things that had happened in the past – things that only I would know about.

Before I left Eileen, she gave me a healing crystal, which she told me to take everywhere I go. After spending a few hours with Eileen, I left her house feeling on top of the world and my knee felt somewhat different, as if it had healed itself. I had no pain and I felt as though I could go onto a park and play football.

The very next day, I went into training and the knee felt great and I had no side effects. In fact, I trained solidly for the next eight weeks without any pain.

Incidentally, I still have that healing crystal and I did take her advice and took it everywhere that I went. I didn't need to go and see Eileen again after that session.

For someone like me who went there with an open mind and had to be convinced, to come out 'healed', I can't describe how that experience felt, and still can't explain it. She was something special and I was very grateful to her. She'd got me, absolutely got me!

Any footballer will say the same thing, that you have to be mentally strong when you get injured as there are a lot of things that go through your mind; you have let down the manager; you've let down the fans; you then have the disappointment of being out of the team for a long time. Then, you start to wonder if you'll ever get back into the team once you're fit again. It's no wonder that footballers, or any athlete, have real issues at times. Although you get used to getting injured, you just wish you could shake it off and carry on playing. I guess a lot of injuries are caused by the player himself, pushing the body to the limit all the time in order to improve themselves. I'm not surprised some footballers play through the pain barrier.

***

Even though my first season at Molineux was over before it began, through injury, Graham proved to be a success at Wolves; he led us to a fourth-place finish in Division One and that meant a play off place, although we lost out to Bolton Wanderers and squandered our chance of promotion. In the second season, despite Wolves being one of the favourites for promotion, the 1995 - 1996 season proved disastrous for the gaffer. After managing just four wins in 16 games, he resigned on 13 November 1995. It was a difficult period of time for me, seeing Graham leave and him not being able to see me in my prime. I felt sorry for Graham at Wolves because a lot of his big signings, including myself, had been injured at some point during that season. For me, to not be able to kick a ball in anger for Graham was heart-breaking. I was gutted and I told him so. Graham was philosophical as ever and conceded it was "part and parcel of football."

Mark McGhee became Wolves manager on 13 December 1995, bringing his assistant, Colin Lee, along with him, after a period under caretaker manager, Bobby Downes. The club's hopes of promotion lay in tatters at the time after just five wins from their previous 21 games under Graham and the start of McGhee's career wasn't that much better.

To say I didn't warm to Mark McGhee is an understatement. He was a complete contrast to Graham Taylor. When he took charge of Wolves, he'd tell me during training that I was in his plans and I'd be playing out wide, left or right. However, by the time the team-sheet was read out on a Friday, my name wasn't even down as a sub. That happened, not just once, but consistently. All I wanted to do was to play football for Wolves. I'd missed most of my Wolves career through injury and now, here was a new manager, with new ideas and he was messing with me.

It was doing my head in!

It was evident after a while McGhee had a problem with the senior players; me, Bully, Don Goodman and Dean Richards included. There was always an ongoing battle with the senior players and the manager, and to this day, I don't know what his problem was. Funnily enough, Froggy liked McGhee and tells me he was good as gold with him, but with me he was the total opposite. I wasn't the only player at the club who didn't get on with him, so I knew it wasn't personal.

We went on a pre-season tour to Austria and Germany and I was playing catch-up again, trying to get back to fitness after yet another injury at the back-end of the previous season. The training went well and I was feeling good. However, I picked up what was to become the most serious injury that I ever had, a ruptured patellar tendon. The patellar injury hit me hard, not only physically, but mentally. Mark McGhee and I didn't see eye-to-eye and he left me to fend for myself in Germany. He never communicated with me whatsoever to see how I was; no phone calls to see how I was, nothing, and that upset me. The players, as expected, were brilliant and I had the backing from them, 100%, but McGhee forgot about me for, not only the whole of the tour, but what seemed like the whole of that season. It was a sad affair and it got me down.

Some players have 'their type of manager' – Mark McGhee just wasn't mine. Ok, I was just getting over yet another major injury, but I could tell McGhee didn't favour me. With managers, it's always the case that you either get on with them or you don't. Mark McGhee would never look me in the eye and be honest with me and at that time I wasn't involved in the first team, but I was getting to a stage where I was training hard and I was desperate to play. I said to McGhee, "If you don't play me I'd rather go out on loan and kick-start my career again." I was probably being a bit ambitious, especially as only two weeks previously I wasn't kicking a ball. However, he promised me I was in his thoughts for a first team recall.

It just didn't happen!

I knew my time was up at Wolves because of the clash I had with the manager. As it happened, Graham Taylor told me he had already contacted Mark McGhee about me joining him at Watford on loan, where he'd just got the manager's job for the second time, shortly after leaving Wolves. Graham told me to keep it quiet and he promised to speak to McGhee again.

Three weeks had passed and I'd heard nothing further about the loan move. I called Graham again and he said McGhee hadn't contacted him. I then went to speak to McGhee about why, after four weeks, I wasn't playing in the first team. I wasn't even playing in the reserves and was nowhere near the first team, so I wasn't happy with that. McGhee again told me he'd "look after" me. He then opened his desk drawer and produced a team sheet and my name was on it for the next game. I then confronted him about the proposed loan move to Watford and he said nobody had contacted him, which I knew wasn't true, as Graham had told me he HAD contacted McGhee.

Anyone who knows me will realise that I haven't got a reputation for being a 'bad boy' so I couldn't understand why he was lying to me. I will go on record and say that I don't feel Mark McGhee was a nice person to me, nor a good manager. That was the day I lost total respect for him and I realised that my days as a Wolves player were numbered.

During that meeting McGhee told me that I was going to be involved in the next game on the Saturday. I took the news well and became a bit excited but at the same time, a little bit hesitant, because I'd heard it all before.

Come the Saturday, guess what? I wasn't in the squad.

After that game, I knocked on McGhee's door again and asked what was going on and told him I wanted to go out on loan. He categorically said he didn't want me out on loan. By this time, I was getting a bit wound up and asked him straight, "You're not going to play me, are you?" Again, he showed me the team sheet for the next game and I was on it. This time, though, I was on the subs bench, although I didn't get on.

Even worse was to follow. McGhee, knowing I was a Villa fan

and ex-Villa player, even left me out of a cup game with them - and I was fit during that period as well. Knowing I wouldn't be playing, he made me travel the short distance to Villa Park with the squad but left me out of the game completely. I would have accepted being on the bench, but I didn't even make that. There was no reason why he couldn't play me because I had played the week before. There was no explanation from McGhee, either. Sitting it out in the stand all by myself at Villa Park killed me – and killed my Wolves career, which to be fair, hadn't really got started. It was the ultimate disappointment, not playing against your old team, especially a team that I had a long association with and supported. For a manager to do that is wrong in my book and it really annoyed me.

I must admit that Mark McGhee's playing style didn't favour the way I played, so maybe that had something to do with why he didn't pick me, but he wasn't honest about it. Leaving me out of the squad at Villa Park wasn't down to my performances, I just think he did it to p*** me off and to prove a point – it was personal. I have a problem when it becomes personal, or seems to be personal, and that's how I found it with Mark McGhee. I'd rather have a manager talk to me and tell me to my face that I don't fit into their plans, and if a club comes in for me, then I can leave on loan or on a permanent deal. Players will accept that – I would, but McGhee just never said that to me. All he seemed to do was string me along and promise me I was in his thoughts when in reality he hardly played me. I'd rather a manager say something like, "I don't fancy you as a player, you're not my cup of tea, do things the right way and try and get yourself a loan." I have no problem with a manager saying something along those lines, but every time he spoke to me he talked to me as though I was his best player and couldn't wait for me to come back from injury – but I knew after a while that wasn't the case. I can take not being picked but when someone says that I was going to play and then I don't even feature in the squad it was inexcusable!

I eventually confronted McGhee about being left out. I didn't go there 'effing and jeffing' but did say something like, "Do you see a future for me at this club? I want to get some games under my belt and prove I'm fit. If I can't do it here, can I go out on loan?" McGhee told me there and then that I was too good a player and he didn't want to send me out on loan. He promised me again that I'd be playing games soon. Week-after-week I knocked his door and asked the same thing, but nothing happened. That went on for about four to six weeks. The time finally came when I just washed my hands of the situation and didn't bother going to confront him again.

People ask me from time-to-time how do footballers deal with being left out of the team when a manager doesn't fancy them. For me, I just kept training at 100% and tried to convince the manager that I was worth picking. I remained professional during that frustrating period and my head never once went down. Some players do the opposite but I never once showed my frustration at not being picked, week after week.

It was quite clear that McGhee wasn't going to pick me.

Not once did I 'slag off' Mark McGhee or the club. I didn't want to cause a scene – that's not my style, and I didn't want to throw my toys out of the pram, but I did make it quite clear that I wanted to play football.

That was the last straw for me!

I wasn't the only player to have had bad experiences with Mark McGhee. Players talk in and out of the dressing room and I found out that both Don Goodman and Dean Richards, two top pros and great players, had similar stories and so did Steve Bull. In contrast, my best mate Froggy was McGhee's type of player, so he was picked for a lot of McGhee's squads and did really well under his managership.

I only played a handful of games under McGhee – it was a really low period in my football career. I remember playing a game at home, the team wasn't playing great and the fans were moaning. It was a very cold miserable night and I wasn't having the best of games. For the first time in my career, I remember not wanting to receive a pass from my teammates for fear of failure. As I came off the pitch at the end of game I said to Froggy that was the first and LAST time that I had felt that way in a game. I knew for certain that my time at Wolves was at an end.

I was coming to the end of my contract at Wolves and had to see out my time because of McGhee's stubbornness and lack of communication. During the summer of 1998, I was released by Wolves after playing just over 20 games for the club in four years. It wasn't the Wolves career that I was hoping for.

CHAPTER 6
Into The Hornet's Nest

"Moving away from home for the first time was hard."

I WAS AT A CROSSROADS in my career. I'd just had four years at Wolves but only played 21 games and had several major injuries – who was going to take me on now? I had interest from Graham Taylor at Watford while I was still at Wolves but nothing materialised. And then I had the chance to play abroad, in Malta of all places!

How it happened was a bit unusual. My eventual ex-mother-in-law, who was Maltese, found out that a club called Birkirkara wanted me to play a small part in their European qualifying games in return for a fee of £20,000. In other words, they wanted me to play two games for £10,000 a game. It was a hell of a lot of money in those days.

My adviser and best friend, John Sharma, and I flew from Birmingham Airport to catch the flight to Valetta with the Maltese airline, Air Malta. While we were still on the ground, the captain announced that we had an engine fault. I looked at John, who was sweating profusely, took my healing crystal (given to me by Eileen Drewery) out of my pocket and clenched it in my hand. John, then said to me, "What are you doing, Dales?" He couldn't understand why I was gripping this rose quartz crystal. I told John the story of where I got it from but I still think he thought I was having a laugh!

After a 50-minute delay, we eventually took off and arrived in Malta, three and half hours later. I'll always remember arriving at the airport because our driver spelt my name, 'Toni'; we had a car waiting for us at the airport and the driver held up a sign with my (mis-spelt) name on! We were driven to a very nice hotel to unpack and then driven to meet the Chairman of the club at the stadium to look around the facilities. We then sat down and talked about my future and what he wanted to do with the football club. At first, the deal was only for those two games, but they then spoke about wanting me to play in the league for that season.

After the formality of talking about my proposed deal, the chairman drove us to a local night club, where I was announced over the PA system and people started clapping; they were obviously very pleased that I was interested in coming to their club. I must admit that it turned out to be a good night. In the early hours of the next morning, John and I couldn't find our hotel – not that we knew the name of it anyway. I think we ended up walking around the town for a good hour and ended up at a kebab place. That, in itself, was bizarre because I normally didn't drink and I didn't particularly like kebabs. Suddenly, while we were waiting for our order, with no idea where we would go next, John realised that the hotel was right opposite us. It was very funny, but sheer madness!

Although Birkirkara made me feel very welcome and put an attractive offer in front of me, the move just didn't feel right for me. I had to think about my family and my career. I felt there was still unfinished business at home, and I wanted a shot at playing in England. I felt that it would be so much more difficult securing a contract back home if I took this short-term deal.

***

I decided to give Graham Taylor a call and he asked me to come down to Watford for a chat where we talked informally in his office at Vicarage Road for what seemed ages. We initially reminisced about the Villa days and his time at Wolves. Both England and Wolves had scarred him, but Graham appeared more relaxed and like himself as I had known him during our time together at Villa. He told me that he had already spoken to the powers that be about signing me, but even though I was a free agent, my injury record was of concern. He did, however, offer me the chance to train during the six-week pre-season to prove my fitness, which

I was happy to do. This time the only obstacle stopping me from joining Watford and reuniting with Graham was my right knee. I had no one telling me that I couldn't go as I was a free agent.

It was the usual Graham Taylor pre-season, running up and down hills to prove fitness.

Luckily, I didn't need a medical so there was no drama with any doctors, like I'd had with the Wolves deal as I was only on a short-term deal. The deal only provided me with expenses – there was no salary as such as I was only there to prove my fitness with a view to getting a playing deal. It was hard for me, in terms of proving my fitness and trying to stay fit. My knee was far from perfect but I was diligent in my preparation for each and every session; I would be at the training ground an hour before any other player arrived doing my pre-activation exercises and strength work. My fitness levels were still very good and I was near the top of most of the testing stats. Although I found nursing my knee through pre-season very tough, I came through it unscathed. The pre-season went well and I must have impressed because Graham offered me the chance to sign on an initial six-month deal. The salary wasn't great but it offered me a chance to play football and to prove my worth.

The downside was that I had to stay away from home for large parts of that season. It was my first real spell away from home in the West Midlands so that aspect was different for me. At first, I stayed in a hotel but eventually moved into digs in the Bush Hill area of Watford with another player, Nick Wright. It was a lovely place to be, run by a lovely old lady called Anne – but it wasn't home.

I was having problems with my marriage before I went to play for Watford, but the move put even more strain on it. Maybe it was a good thing in one way, leaving the bad things that were going on at the time behind me, but I didn't really want to leave my kids for days on end. However, it was what I did for a living and I had to go where the work was and in this case it was in Watford. I was concerned about my kids and the affect that it had on them by being away from home most of the week. Playing for Villa and Wolves meant I lived at home and saw my wife and kids daily, but moving to digs in Watford meant I had to go back and forth to the West Midlands weekly when we had a break in the training routine. I tried to get home once or twice a week if I could and I travelled by train rather than car, so as not to tire myself out by driving up and down the M1 and M6.

It was tough in terms of my mental wellbeing, but it never once affected my training. In fact, the opposite applied. Training and playing in games helped me in a positive way – it was a release from my marital problems, but the hard part was when I was at my digs alone and I had time to think about those issues.

Family has always been the most important thing in my life – and I not only include my two kids but my dog too. I always tried to find time for my kids; football is a game where you have time on your hands in between games and training. I wasn't interested in snooker, golf, tennis, darts or going on the p*** after training. As soon as the football was finished, I went home to see my kids, and Sebastian, my Golden Retriever. I wasn't a great doggy person at first, but the kids convinced me to get a dog. In hindsight, he turned out to be a godsend. Given that Michelle wanted a dog as well, I was always going to lose that argument.

At first, when he was a puppy Sebastian was a nightmare. We couldn't handle him. He wrecked the house when we were out, and he hated being left alone on his own even for five minutes. In the end we had to take him to a professional training school and he came back a different dog. However, he had his moments. One time, I took him to the Bodymoor Heath training ground during pre-season and let him off the lead (big mistake) and he ran after every ball that was kicked.

Having said that, he was a godsend, both with my kids and for myself. When I'd take him for a walk and I needed a bit of time to myself away from humans, he was good non-human company. He really helped me mentally as well.

Sebastian lived to the ripe old ageof 17 and we were all devastated when we lost him.

Football was my escape from my personal troubles. I'm the type of person who needs to be doing something. I need something to occupy my mind. Football was EVERYTHING to me back then. I couldn't bear not playing. Whenever I was injured it was really hard for me. I can't describe how awful it was being injured, watching your teammates training and playing is the worse feeling in the world for any footballer. I'd been playing football since the age of seven – it was the only thing I knew. Even playing for Watford, I had the same appetite for the game as I'd had as a kid. Football for me was never a 'job' in a sense. I was so obsessed that even during the off-season I'd be keeping fit by running, strength training and kicking a ball around. I very often got told off by my managers because the idea of the summer break was to rest the body, but I never did that.

***

During the time that I spent in Watford, I made some good friends in Nigel Gibbs and Nick Wright. Nigel would invite me round to his house for dinner occasionally and we'd go to the cinema. However, I found myself on the phone to the kids during most of my spare time. It was tough being away from my young kids.

There were a really good bunch of lads at Watford and a good family-run club. Again, I faced the same old problems with niggling injuries. What I remember mostly was the thigh strain that I was carrying all the way through that season. I had to have a minor operation on my thigh and that kept me out for three or four weeks. I came back from that, but I seem to remember that I had other injuries throughout the season. I always knew I'd have to look after my troublesome knee so I did a lot more strengthening exercises and it became part and parcel of my life. Each training session was a struggle. I was in agony after training and after games, but I somehow managed to get through them. I knew that I was carrying an injury and I had it in the back of my mind that this may be my last season.

By mid-way through the season, I'd got back into my football and was fully fit. We were doing reasonably well in the league, especially at home. With six games to go, we were well off the play-offs and had to win virtually all of our remaining games to stand a chance. We did just that, barring a draw at Barnsley on the penultimate game of the season.

Even before the play-offs, I was thinking about my future as I knew that Graham wasn't looking to keep me at the club. Since leaving Villa, I'd had terrible problems with my knee and it caused me a lot of stress and pain, and a loss of game time. All I wanted to do now was to manage my knee and get through the rest of my career, what little there was of it left.

We had reached the play-offs where we faced Birmingham City over two legs. Graham picked me in the first-leg of the play-off semi-final games against Birmingham City, but I picked up another thigh strain during training. I was desperate to make it for the second-leg tie at St Andrews and it got to the stage that I went to see Graham after that training session and opened up about the injury, telling him that I was struggling. I told him that I could get through the game but I probably wouldn't do myself any justice. It was a difficult thing for me to do, mainly because Graham had meticulously planned the training session and now, here I was telling him that I was struggling after I'd got through 45 minutes of intensive training. I knew how Graham would react, something like, "Why didn't you say something earlier?" It was one of those situations, when you think you've done the right thing, but at the wrong time. Graham wasn't impressed!

For me, I thought I could have got through the training without any harm done to the thigh strain but it didn't work out like that. Graham was angry with me because I was in his plans for the game but told me I'd done the right thing in coming to see him. He said I was brave to tell him.

However, prior to the second leg semi-final tie at St Andrews, something unimaginable happened. I received a threatening phone call from a so-called Birmingham City fan. My (then) wife, Michelle answered the phone and the person was really abusive, saying that if I turned up for the game they would cut my throat. How they obtained my home number I will never know, but we had to get the police involved immediately. It was a frightening time of my life and unfortunately, my then wife copped the brunt of it.

Unfortunately, the police didn't manage to catch the abuser.

I haven't mentioned that story before and it was kept hush-hush by the club at the time – I didn't want it out in the public domain and I still believe that was the right thing to do.

We did beat Birmingham (on penalties) after losing the second-leg 1 – 0 to reach the final. As a consequence of my thigh strain, I missed out on the final as well.

It wasn't the only time that I had been given verbal abuse by Birmingham City fans. Playing for Watford in a league game at St Andrews in April 1999, I was the brunt of the supporters' abuse, being the ex-Villa player of course. I soon shut them up as I created our first goal for Tommy Mooney and I scored our second with a rare header as we went on to win 2 – 1 in front of a big crowd. That was a very good day and I really cherished the score-line and my own performance. I didn't 'milk' my celebrations but held my arms aloft in front of the Blues' fans – that was enough to keep them quiet. I was more interested in celebrating with my teammates rather than goading the home fans. It was something I never got involved in if I'm honest – I would much rather make my feet do the talking.

Even though I wasn't involved in the final itself, I travelled down to Wembley with the lads and was involved with the celebrations after our 2 – 0 win against Bolton. That day wasn't without its problems as I had to be escorted by the police, before, during and after the game, following what had happened prior to the Blues game. As I was travelling back to Birmingham the following day the police thought that it was precautionary.

I did get a medal which was some sort of a consolation. The following day, I was also involved in the open-top bus tour of Watford town centre, which was amazing.

Although I didn't play at Wembley, Graham made sure that I was involved in everything, for which I was very grateful. Then, literally a day after that final, Graham told me that my contract wasn't being renewed. I'd only played a dozen or so games for the Hornets so that news didn't really come as any surprise. I told Graham that I was very grateful to him that he had showed faith in me for that season and I was proud to have played my part and helped Watford gain promotion. We shook hands and parted our ways for the third time – well, fourth if you include England.

I was nearly 32 and had no club. It was at that time that I really contemplated retirement for the first time in my football career. Injuries had hampered me throughout my career and at my age it wouldn't get any easier. It couldn't continue like that. I couldn't keep getting niggling injuries, having operations and keep receiving pain-killing injections just to help me through games.

CHAPTER 7
Keeping the Dream Alive

*"I wanted to prolong my playing career after losing so much
of it through injury."*

I'D JUST SHAKEN Graham Taylor's hand for the last time. I
was club-less and no idea what I would be doing during the long
summer and pre-season until some foreign clubs came in for
me. One offer, in particular, was to play In Israel of all places.

I received a call from the ex-Liverpool forward, Ronny
Rosenthal, who I'd played with at Watford. He told me about
some clubs (I can't remember the names of the clubs) in Israel
who were interested in signing me on a short-term deal. I needed
to play football somewhere and thought that it would now be an
interesting proposition to play abroad.

I agreed to go out to Tel Aviv and speak to these three clubs.
However, before I flew out, Ronny gave me a letter he'd written
and said, "If you get any problems getting through Customs,
then show them this letter." I thought it a bit strange at the time
but went along with it.

So, as I tried to get through Customs at Tel Aviv Airport I was
stopped and the official asked me several questions about the
purpose of my visit and questions about my family. I told him
that I was in the country to join a football club but he wasn't
convinced and said the information that I'd given him wasn't
sufficient, so he refused me entry. The Customs official said he
may have to search me and 'interrogate' me more. It was at that
point that I remembered I had the letter Ronny had given me, so
I handed it to the official. The conversation was starting to get a

bit heated and I was becoming frustrated, but after he read the letter, he let me enter the country. I hadn't read the letter myself but it must have stated who I was and what I was doing in the country and coming from Ronny, it obviously held some weight. Ronny was an absolute icon in Israel and he must have known that I'd have faced some interrogation at the airport. Whatever Ronny had written was enough to convince the Customs official that I was a right and proper person.

Once I got myself settled into the hotel, I had a couple of training sessions at the first club but from day one, the place didn't feel right. One incident I will always remember was when I was getting changed for training, I heard a massive explosion. I literally jumped out of my skin but when I looked around the changing room, none of the other players took any notice. I asked one of the lads what had happened and he said it was a Palestinian bomb but they were all used to it. After that, I just wanted to get back home.

I'd only been there for three days but I already knew that Israel wasn't for me. It was just as well because I would have struggled with my knee.

I was home at last after my foreign adventure, but I'd always known Walsall were interested in signing me. Throughout my career, and throughout my life in general, I would always adapt to change and that's just what I did following that season at Watford. I was good at adapting to change – nothing ever fazed me. I didn't mind playing for a top club like Villa, or a lower league club like Walsall. As a footballer, I think you have to have that mindset.

Walsall were managed by former Villa winger Ray Graydon and he had told Graham Taylor before I left Watford that he wanted me at Bescot on a six-month contract. That was before my foreign adventure though, so I contacted Ray and had a chat about playing for him at Walsall. Life, as they say, sometimes doesn't go the way you expect. It has lots of twists and turns and sometimes an unusual path can be the thing that changes your life – for better or for worse.

About a week later I had a conversation with Ray, and I was quite honest with him about my situation with my knee. Ray was also honest with me as he told me if things weren't right for both parties after three months then he said we would call it a day. In other words, if my knee wasn't right he would have to let me go.

Playing for Walsall meant I could be at home with the kids. However, my life then was heading in a different direction on a personal level. I was joining a club back in the West Midlands, so I was as excited for the season to start as any season previously, regardless of the club I was with. As I said, I was adaptable but all I wanted to do was to play football. I was very thankful to Ray for showing an interest in me. Ray told me that he thought it was a good club for me to play for. He suggested I could really help the younger players, being the experienced player in the group.

If Graham Taylor was pretty regimental in what he did and his dress code, then Ray was in the same strict mould – no jeans, no scruffy tee-shirts, only smart clothes were allowed. Anyone who has seen my wardrobe of clothes will understand those rules were OK for me. While I was fine with that, Ray also told me to get my hair cut, to which I replied, "Ray, I'll do anything for you, but that's never going to happen." To be fair, Ray chuckled and he accepted that my haircut won't ever affect the way I play. He was fine with that.

Walsall were a friendly club and had not long moved into their new home, The Bescot Stadium. However, they hadn't got a training ground so we had to move from place to place – we even trained for a period at Lilleshall, the old England training ground. It was a right pain because it was a good 25 miles away.

It was about three months into the season, or maybe a bit more than that, when I had a conversation with Ray we agreed to rip up the contract. I was struggling. My knee just wasn't in a good way, although I did manage about a half dozen games for the Saddlers. It was a case of feeling fantastic one day, but the next I felt like an old man who'd been shot in the knee. I came on as a substitute for the last 15 minutes against Wolves, which was one of my last games for Walsall; I felt good and was having a good game, but I knew then that a cameo appearance here or there wasn't going to be enough and that my days were numbered. It was then that the word 'retirement' was high up in my vocabulary. I knew things were only going to become harder and I couldn't expect a club the size of Walsall to carry me and nurse me through the whole season.

I was also thinking about my own life. I wanted a career after playing football – I didn't want to be in a wheelchair for the rest of my life just because I kept prolonging my playing career. I decided to call it a day. Walsall were my last league club.

Unfortunately for the Saddlers, they were relegated at the end of that season (1999 – 2000).

So, I found myself a free agent yet again and although I wasn't looking for new opportunities, just contemplating retirement, the opportunity to play in China came along. In those days, the Chinese league wasn't established like it is today, it was raw and hardly any foreign footballers were playing in the league. Again, the offer came via Ronny Rosenthal and I ventured out to China, although I can't remember the name of the club.

When I got to China, I immediately took a dislike to the place. I don't know what it was about it but something put me right off. Anyway, I agreed to go to the trial at the club. I say trial, it was nothing to do with football. What I had to do was to prove that I was fit enough to play in their league by doing what's called the Cooper Test, a 12-minute run around a track to check aerobic fitness. If you pass the test, you can play in the Chinese football league. It's that simple. I undertook the test, along with another 50-odd players. I passed the test and then started to train with the lads the next day.

I think I lasted two days when I phoned Ronny, asking him to sort out a flight to come back home. However, it proved difficult to sort out some flights to get back, given that the club had paid for my return flights, so I had to continue to train while the flights were sorted out. I think that lasted another five days before I boarded the flight back to the UK.

China wasn't for me, but it was an experience to say the least.

I knew that this was the time to start looking seriously at my future career and there was only one path I wanted to follow, and that was to be a fitness coach. Ever since I picked up my first serious injury back in 1994, I knew that there would have to be a life after football and I had looked at a future as a fitness coach. My ideal scenario was to have packed up playing at Wolves at the age of 34, but that obviously didn't materialise, so I had to think how to prolong my playing days for as long as I could before I made the move into fitness coaching.

I was without a club again but the difference this time was that I knew what I wanted to do and that was to go back to university full-time to do a Sports Science degree. If memory serves me right, I finished at Walsall in the October of 1999 and immediately enrolled at university onto the second year of the course at Coventry University. I was already doing an HND (Higher National Diploma) course, which I'd passed, so I was allowed to join the second year of the degree. It was a move that I was always going to do but leaving Walsall motivated me to push forward with my plans.

Sometimes things happen out of the blue and it was around this time that non-League club, Forest Green Rovers' manager, Frank Gregan, telephoned me and asked me if I wanted to play for them. At that time, Forest Green had just recruited my old mate Dave Norton, whom I played with at Villa back in the day. I must admit, it was a move that I'd never considered – to play for a non-league team, but I agreed to meet Frank at the club in deepest Gloucestershire. I wanted assurances on how the club was run and why they were struggling in the league. Frank talked about the club (which he had managed for the previous five years) and what he wanted to do with it. It was a club that was struggling to attract fans, with their attendances around the 600 – 800 mark every home game. I was honest with Frank and explained the situation with my knee and the fact that I had enrolled on a university course, but I think that suited him as they only trained twice a week so it wasn't as though I needed to be at the club full-time. Training was on Tuesday and Thursday evenings, so that seemed to fit in with my course. When he mentioned the wages, I agreed to join Forest Green. Although it wasn't the money that the decision was made on, when they said I'd earn double what I was on at Walsall that was a plus for me.

It seemed that I had made the right decision, one that I could fit in everything I wanted and where I wanted to be at that time in my life – to be paid for playing football, to study and to live at home. It was a win-win situation for me.

Being at university full-time, I would travel down to the club on a Tuesday and Thursday afternoon, when I'd leave Coventry University at 4:30pm and get to training at around 6:30pm, start training at 7:30pm and finish at 9:30pm, and I'd get home by 11pm. It was a long day and hard work but I was doing two things I loved. Even though I was only training twice a week and playing once a week in a non-league team, it was still a struggle with regards my knee. I had to make sure that I didn't overdo the training so Thursday's session was only a light one. I had to manage my knee extremely carefully. In my second season there it became less of a problem, as I was doing more fitness work rather than playing as I had become a part-time player/fitness coach, and that worked out particularly nicely for me.

I won't lie – the standard of football in the Conference was better than I thought it would be – I was quite surprised at the quality. With the influx of foreign players into the Premier League and Division One (second tier) the quality seemed to filter down the leagues so that brought the standard of the lower leagues up.

However, my debut was pretty unforgettable. We had an away game at Sutton United, so I had to drive down to Forest Green on the Friday to sign contracts, stay in a hotel, then drive to Surrey to play in the game the next day. I arrived for the 3pm kick-off with half-an-hour to spare and during that time, I had to meet the lads, shake everyone's hand and get changed. When I got on the field I didn't know anyone – I'd only literally met my teammates in the changing room, but that didn't stop me flying past one player, beating another and another. For a split second I began to think this league is easy. . . until I met a huge centre-half who clattered into me and stopped me in my tracks, and I crashed to the ground. I stared up at him and he 'attempted' to pick me up off the ground, squeezing my arms so hard they nearly popped! He whispered close to ear, "Welcome to the Conference!"

Looking back at my time as a player I played against some very hard men and still have the scars to prove it – and a season-ticket in the physio room. So, to be introduced to the Conference like that didn't frighten me one bit!

By far the dirtiest player I played against would have been Julian Dicks when he was at West Ham. He would kick me every time I had the ball – and even when I didn't! He was tough to play against because he never spoke or verbally abused me. He would, out of the blue, elbow me in the ribs or knee me on the back of my legs when the ball was on the other side of the pitch. He was horrible to play against but he never fazed me. I soon learned at a very young age with my pace that the only way for defenders to stop me was to kick me – and that's what they did and probably the main reason why I picked up so many injuries. In the end I took this as a compliment and it gave me a boost, more than it did a hindrance.

Talking to my teammates who came from clubs that I played

against the team talk given by the opposition coach to their defenders about me was to "kick him early and get in his face so he won't want to know." This couldn't be further from the truth. I became incredibly adept at riding tackles and blanking out abuse. I remember getting cleaned out waist-high by Mark Dennis when he was at Southampton. He leaned over me and said, "next time you're going to be carried off on a f****** stretcher." My reply was simply to giggle at him and tell him that he would have to try and catch me first. He was enraged that firstly I didn't bite and get into a slanging match with him and also the fact that it really didn't bother me what he said. Bravery on the field not only comes from diving into a fifty- fifty tackle or putting your head in where you know it may get booted; bravery can be shown when you are going to kicked and still demand the ball to go and take on your opponent. Stuart Pearce was another hard tackling opponent. He certainly lived up to his nickname of 'Psycho'. Yes, he was extremely physical and took no prisoners, but he was fair and had a genuine desire to go and win the ball. If his opponent was in the way then that was collateral damage! I used to enjoy playing against Stuart because you either skipped past him or invariably received a crunching tackle. I also played with Stuart for England and as an established international he took the time to help me settle into the England squad. He was very much the leader off the field in the same way as you saw him on it.

My signing attracted a lot of publicity and this put another 200 on the gate for my home debut.

That was the start of it and it didn't get any easier. I think a lot of ex-professionals go into the lower leagues thinking that it will be a walk in the park, but I can tell you the football is hard and the standard is good. At the time, the facilities weren't the best, although in recent years a lot of non-league clubs have invested in their facilities and Forest Green were no different.

I managed to play around 30 games for Forest Green in the three and half years that I was there. I managed to keep myself fit and didn't have any lasting injuries, maybe a couple of thigh sprains, but nothing major.

During my time at Forest Green, I played with some very familiar lads like Paul Birch, Nigel Spink, Dave Norton (ex-

Villa), Dave Barnett and Dennis Bailey (ex-Birmingham City). In fact, Nigel Spink and Dave Norton took charge of Forest Green for a season when Frank left in 2000. The fact that so many familiar faces were at the club we ended up sharing the driving to and from the West Midlands. It was great working with Birchy again, after all that time of being away from Villa and Wolves. Birchy had actually retired from football in 2000 and got a job as a postman, but was enticed back to be a coach for Forest Green by Nigel Spink.

We were constantly battling relegation and beat it during my time there. The first season, we beat relegation on the final game of the season; I think we needed a draw against all the odds. There was a big celebration after that game as well. The club house at the time was literally behind the goal so all the players were mixing with fans which was nice.

We did reach the final of the FA Trophy in 2001, which was played at Villa Park, of all places, as work was being done to rebuild Wembley Stadium at the time. It was an added bonus, what with the extra meaning it had for me personally because since I'd left Villa I hadn't played at Villa Park, not even for Wolves – and it ended up being the last time that I played there, too. To get the chance to play there was immense, although we were in the away dressing room. We played Canvey Island in the final on 13th May in front of around 10,000 fans. I'd hardly played during that season but I had worked hard to get fit and well for that final. Unfortunately, we lost the game 1 – 0. I think it proved to be my last game for Forest Green as I decided to hang up my boots at the age of 34 after a few seasons as a player.

The following season, I joined the coaching team as a fitness coach under Nigel Spink.

While I was juggling my family life with doing my degree and being a part-time fitness coach at Forest Green, I was also doing some paid work with Villa's youngsters, so it made for a hectic schedule, but one which I certainly enjoyed. Villa were very good to me, and Jim Walker, Villa's physio at the time, let me do a lot of fitness, strength, conditioning and agility work with the Under-10s initially, then I worked with the 15-and 16-year-olds at the academy. I also did some speed and agility work with a young Gabby Agbonlahor and even then, he stood out for me.

He was rapid. I always get asked, was Gabby quicker than me? That's a question I can't answer. I never knew how quick I was in my prime and it's only when I watch myself on YouTube now that I realise how quick I was. I knew when I was a footballer that I could beat anybody at any time over a short distance but that came naturally to me. It's other people's opinion whether I was quicker than Gabby. He was a quiet lad and got his head down. He wanted to improve and he was always destined to make the first team.

Not only that, but there was also the opportunity to do some fitness testing with the first team as well. It all helped.

As it turned out I nearly worked with Graham Taylor (again!) as I had the opportunity to speak to him during that time. It was during his second spell back as Villa manager and I remember him intimating that there might be an opportunity for a role in the Sports Science department once I had qualified for my degree in July 2003. However, he left the club the following season so that was that.

CHAPTER 8
Football, Fitness and Sports Science

"Keeping fit and staying healthy has always been a love of mine."

WHILE I WAS OUT injured with my second big knee injury at Wolves, I had time to think about what I wanted to do when I retired from playing football. I was only 28 years old at the time but I thought that the time had come to start planning my next move. It's probably something most footballers dread, some put it off to the very last minute and some probably don't want to think about it too much. It's not a subject that any footballer wants to think about because all that matters when you're fit and able is playing as much as you can.

My first thought was to be a physiotherapist; I'd already seen more than my fair share of them in my career so far, so why not? I was always interested in how the body worked so the thought of studying biomechanics and physiology of the body and how it works really appealed to me. However, what put me off were the hours they had to put in; looking into a career as a physiotherapist told me that they put in a tremendous amount of work, not that I'm work shy or anything, but I wanted to marry my career with a good family life.

I'd worked with some fantastic physios during my career, people like Jim Walker at Villa, Dave Hancock and Steve Kemp, who's now the lead men's physiotherapist for the England national squad. They are all fantastic at their jobs and fabulous people.

Although I was interested in the workings of the body, my big obsession, ever since I started at Villa as an apprentice, was fitness, so it was a natural progression for me to seek a future career as a fitness coach. I loved the fitness side of training; most footballers hate that side of it, but I was different in that I loved pre-season and all the drills that we had to do in order to stay fit. I was always interested in biomechanics and nutrition; diet was key for me and still is, probably even more so now.

Watching the other guys training and playing football on a Saturday was heart-breaking for me; I just wanted to play every week, but injuries took their toll on my body. While I was injured I looked at ways of manipulating my body functionally, but also aesthetically. I started to take on a bit of a body shape and I wanted to keep that for as long as I could. As an injured sportsman it's easy to pile the weight on when you're inactive, not necessarily through over-eating, but simply through not training or not training with the same intensity as normal. Even if a player ate the same amount of food while injured, the reason why some put weight on is because they don't train or don't train as hard.

That wasn't going to happen to me, and I made it my prerogative to keep my body shape and to keep myself as fit as I could during the times that I was injured and could still do exercise. Even during my several spells of injury at Wolves I was looking at ways of manipulating my diet, whether through eating or supplementation. I was fascinated with diet and fitness so I started to read up about it and spoke to several physios and people in the know to try and get a good understanding of the subject.

By the time I was 29 and going through my third or fourth major operation at Wolves, I knew what I wanted to be when I hung my boots up; I wanted to be a Sports Scientist or a Fitness Coach for a football club. I knew I'd have to take the plunge and go to university to study Sports Science so I knew that it wouldn't be an easy passage for me, but it was something I really wanted to pursue.

My obsession with fitness, and especially strength training started during my first year as a professional footballer at Villa. Strength training at that time wasn't really a big deal; you had the usual dumb-bells and medicine balls, etc., but it wasn't really taken seriously. The only time we did weights was about a month before the season ended and we called those 'beach weights', ready for the holiday season – that's how seriously we took it.

I was introduced to a strength and conditioning trainer called Tony Ford, who was the 'un-official' fitness coach at Villa. It was rare back then for footballers to see coaches away from the day-to-day training; I saw Tony to supplement my football training. I wasn't alone though, as a few of the other Villa lads used to see Tony at his gym as well. It was a great introduction to strength and conditioning for me; I absolutely loved it, probably because it was something we didn't do at the club and I wanted to learn more about it. I didn't love it because of the aesthetic side of it, it was more to help me to become stronger, as I was such a small, wiry player, I wanted to beef up a bit to help my presence on the pitch. Although I was quick and agile, I wanted it to help me kick off my football career and give me something 'extra'.

As time went on, the training with Tony at his private gym did add something to my game; it added not only strength, but power to my already lightning pace. Tony Ford was a great character and motivated me to become this 'new' player. Tony must have been about 60 at the time but he had pedigree; he won a weightlifting gold medal for England at the 1974 Commonwealth Games in New Zealand. Even at that age, he was a machine, and wouldn't take any nonsense from his clients (or anyone). When you trained with him, you trained 100%; it was tough but it was absolutely fantastic.

Fitness and strength training soon became part of my life and my daily routine, together with football. However, it wasn't until I went to Wolves that my calling came. During the time before the start of that first season with Wolves, I was almost living in my local David Lloyd Fitness Centre, trying to get fit, strong and agile for the season ahead. It was devastating for me personally, and also for my friends and teammates, that I picked up that serious injury, because before that game I was so looking forward to the season ahead. Having picked up the first of my serious injuries in the first pre-season game, it was a very hard thing to take in. I say that, because when I left Villa in the summer of 1994, I was the fittest I'd ever been in my whole career, either before or subsequently; I was super-fit and at my peak. Looking back at my records (which I've kept all this time) I was doing 5 km in 19 minutes, which is some going – those were the 'good old days'.

The injury came from absolutely nowhere and I wasn't prepared for doing nothing; I have an OCD in terms of the time I spend away from football, which was my life and meant everything to me, so not being able to play football came as a devastating shock. I had to do something during the time I had post-op, so I decided to substitute playing, with the bike and rowing machines at the Wolves training ground. I also used the time to pump iron and that was the thing that kept me sane. I was obsessed to stay as fit as I could, even though I wasn't able to run or kick a ball.

As I've said already, it was a long, long four years at Wolves, what with the injuries that I sustained and constantly trying to get fit. That routine of bike, rowing machines and pumping iron became a regular occurrence. I wasn't alone in my pursuit of fitness because I had friends in Geoff Thomas, Steve Bull, Don Goodman and Froggy himself, who were injured during stages of those four years, so it turned out to be a bit of a 'gym club'. Don't get me wrong, it didn't replace going out there kicking a ball around and playing in front of 30,000 at Molineux, but it was my substitute and my saviour.

I often wonder how I would compare in terms of fitness to the modern-day footballer. As a winger, I had to be one of the fittest players on the pitch. How lucky are the footballers of today, with all the equipment and support that they have at their disposal; all the luxury training facilities; all the manicured pitches they play on and all the backroom staff to look after them. They are so, so lucky – I'd have loved to have had all of those 'tools' in my day. Every team today has specialist coaches; fitness coaches, striker coaches, defence coaches, you name it, they have it, but we just had 'the coach', or maybe if we were lucky, two coaches.

Training day in, day out was brilliant. I loved training as much as I loved playing on a Saturday afternoon and would give as much every day of the week as I did for those 90 minutes on a matchday. I didn't really have a weakness when it came to fitness and the stats backed it up. I would be in the top three for endurance, speed, agility strength and jump tests. However, some of my teammates hated training; you'll find lots of footballers, even today hate training, they just want to play games but it's all part of being a professional footballer.

And of course, one or two players didn't train at all.

There's always one or two players who give an extra 10% (if there is such a thing) and I was the one who would stay behind and did extra training; I trained at 100 % every session because I wanted to improve myself, so the only way I was going to do that was to train – and to train hard. It wasn't only football training I loved, but I was also a fitness fanatic. I wanted to be fit and stay fit; I had to be fit for my job on the pitch, for sure, but I actually enjoyed it, which was half the battle.

***

In May 2003, I spoke to Dave Kelly who was Assistant to Neil Warnock at Sheffield United and he said that they were looking for a fitness coach. Dave suggested that I give Neil a call to discuss the role, which I did. I spoke to Neil and said I was looking to apply for the vacant role as the first team fitness coach and would love the opportunity to work for him. Neil said he had someone in mind and intimated that I may have called him a bit late. However, he said he would think about it and get back to me. About two hours later, Neil called, true to his word, and invited me to go down to see him the next day. He told me to bring my training gear as he wanted to watch me take a training session at a local college at 12pm.

It was a three-and-a-half-hour drive and when I arrived, it looked as though Neil had been meticulous in organising a bunch of college kids and I had to put a fitness session on for around 10 – 15 kids. After about half-an-hour, Neil had seen enough and we went back to his house for lunch and a chat about the role. Neil said he was concerned that I was too quietly spoken and asked me how I would cope if players started giving me grief. I replied, "They won't give me grief. I'll get the job done – there's no problem there. I may have a smile on my face but I'm ruthless in my work and I'll get the job done." I told Neil that I would earn the respect of players because not only have I played the game, but I was also very good at my job – and that is something that I still believe. Neil then asked me what I would do if players gave me backchat, to which I replied, "Backchat? Players backchat all the time – it's part and parcel of the game, I've been there, done it and got the t-shirt – I can handle myself." I went on to explain that being an ex-player, I knew what players needed with regard to football, and I applied Sports Science to fit the footballer. It's important to have the qualifications to help move the club forward in terms of performance but understanding the 'language' of players; for instance, when to push them, when to lay off, during a tough Championship season.

By the time I got home at 8pm, Neil called me to tell me that I had got the job. To this day, I still don't know who the other candidate was.

So, after Neil giving me a bit of a hard time in the 'interview' I started the new role of Fitness Coach at Sheffield United during the pre-season of the 2003 – 2004 season. United were in the Division One (second tier) after finishing third in the league and coming runners' up in the Play-Off Final.

Neil Warnock was the ideal manager to start my career as a fitness coach. I'd just graduated from Coventry University (in May 2003) so it was the ideal environment for me to learn on the job. The term 'learn on your feet' springs to mind, and for me, that was ideal and I will be forever grateful to Neil for the opportunity. Not only that, but Neil also gives his staff the freedom to get on with their jobs without constant interference because he trusts them to do their job. As the fitness coach, I knew my field whereas Neil stayed in his lane and he let me get on with what I do best. Needless to say, I took to the job like a duck to water. I knew I would. Being a player helped me in my new role for sure. The one thing that being an ex-player brought me was empathy with the players, but not only that, I had the science to back it up. I knew I could get the best out of the players – which was exactly what I said to Neil.

There was one incident that I will never forget where Neil caned me and I mean caned me, when I put on a training session for the lads that he didn't like. Neil was raging after this particular training session, to the extent that there was spit coming out of his mouth as he was shouting at me – he lost his rag big time. That was in the morning, but in the afternoon, after he'd calmed down he talked to me as if nothing had happened a few hours previously. Looking back on that training session, I was a naïve fitness coach who wanted to impress his manager by putting my slant on the plans that he'd laid out for the session. In other words, I agreed to do the session according to his instructions, but I took those plans to another level. In my mind, I was doing what he told me to do, but in another way – in a Sports Science way, not in the Neil Warnock way. The lesson

I learned from that rollocking was, never reinvent your manager's instructions – if he wants something doing in a certain way, do it that way and don't put your own spin on it. Maybe in hindsight, I should have consulted him first but at the time I was new to the role and didn't really know Neil enough to have consulted him – and he didn't know me enough to have trusted my judgement. Conversely, Neil would equally complement me for putting on an excellent session. He was fair in that respect.

Although everyone has been rollocked by their manager from time-to-time, I must say that was the worst caning I ever had; it probably wasn't the last one I had from Neil, although the subsequent canings were over niggly little things. Having said that, I don't remember being rollocked by Mick McCarthy – heated conversations, maybe but never a rollocking. Mick wasn't a baller though, very direct, but I really don't remember him losing his rag at me, or anyone else.

As time went on, I was able to gain the trust of Neil and how to read him and in time, I felt strong enough to give him feedback about things which maybe didn't work well. I soon discovered that the ideal time to speak to Neil was when he was calm and I could then give him some feedback from an ex-player on how to approach a certain scenario. I think Neil appreciated feedback at the right time. There was no benefit to anyone in me feeding back to him when things weren't going well and he was balling at the players. It didn't take long for both of us to understand the way we ticked. I can honestly say that I took on board everything Neil taught me and used the information in my career.

Working with Neil was 'different' in that he'd go home after the game on Saturday and we wouldn't see him until the Tuesday. This was because his family home was so far away from Sheffield at the time. However, he didn't do that at the start, during the time he was getting his staff together and organised. As soon as things fitted into place and he started to trust his staff, he'd leave us for those three days to get on with training without his guidance. He also trusted his players to follow the lead of the coaches who were left in charge.

Of course, there were some players who also lived long distances from the training ground and he allowed them time off to spend with their families, which was another example of him trusting his players. There was never any animosity among the players about why this happened because everyone knew that it was a good thing and the right thing to do and they understood why he did that. It was all about looking after his players, being fair and gaining everyone's respect.

Neil was brilliant at taking the pressure off his players. He'd never go in front of the TV camera and slag his players off. In fact, he always deflected the attention away from them. He'd always take the blame for a poor performance. OK, he'd sometimes slate the referee or the opposition, but he'd always try and take the pressure off his own players and he was a master at doing that.

While Neil's family home was miles from South Yorkshire, I commuted there for those four years from my home in Sutton Coldfield. It was a fairly straight and easy route, up the A38 and M1 and I did that every day. Having said that, the time of day I usually set out there was very little traffic on the road. It took less than an hour and half and I tended to leave home at 05:10 and get to the training ground for 06:30. Obviously, if we had a mid-week game I'd stay in a hotel overnight, but in general I commuted. It was never a chore for me – I enjoyed the drive and enjoyed the training even more so. In fact, I'd go as far as to say I probably enjoyed the sports science aspect of being a fitness coach more than being a footballer, in terms of the work that I did. It was all action and bloody hard work, planning, preparing and putting on the sessions. I was never off work as such because I always had players calling me at all hours of the day. My day didn't finish when I left the training ground.

When I first started there was only me as the fitness coach, but as time went on and I established myself into the role we employed an assistant fitness coach.

One thing that springs to mind when I look back on my time at Bramall Lane is the Carlos Tevez incident that happened during a Premier League game at West Ham in November 2006. Tevez stormed out of the ground at the end of that game after being substituted by Alan Pardew and threw a tantrum as he walked off.

Neil had been at his boyhood club since 1999 but he resigned after the disastrous 2006 – 2007 Premier League relegation season. His main achievements were to guide us into the semi-final of both the League Cup and FA Cup in the 2002 – 2003 season, as well as runners' up in the play-offs, after coming third in the league, not to mention promotion to the Premier League in the 2005 – 2006 season.

There were rumours the day before Neil left that he was facing the sack or was leaving his post, but credit to Neil, he told all of his staff face-to-face on the day that he actually left. It was a pretty sad day for me because Neil was great to work for. He very often got bad press for the style of football he likes his teams to play but I learned so much from him, how to understand people and how to understand other managers. For me, if you can work well under Neil Warnock, you will be equipped to work with anyone.

Bryan Robson took over from Neil for the 2007 – 2008 season in the Championship with the remit to get the club promoted at the first attempt and he immediately brought in Brian Kidd as his assistant. However, I did have a conversation with Bryan after he was appointed and he told me to put my pre-season fitness plan together, which I did and at that stage everything was fine. We got through pre-season and my plan went well for the players.

About a couple of weeks before the season started, Bryan told me that he was getting his own team in, including his own fitness coach. The news was a bit out of the blue – I wasn't really expecting it, especially having taken the pre-season and the plans had been put in place for the season ahead. It came as a shock. Bryan told me it was nothing personal, but he'd worked with the guy before. I subsequently found out that Bryan was just waiting for this guy to be released from his previous post before announcing him at Sheffield United.

There were some false stories doing the rounds at the time that I'd fallen out with Bryan about the club's training methods, or we that we'd had a blazing row, but these were 100% untrue and nonsense. I had no problems with either Bryan Robson, or Brian Kidd, or with their training methods and they were OK to work with, but these things happen in football. A new manager comes in and he wants things done differently, it's part and parcel of football. I was just delighted that having left there, an opportunity arose at Wolves. Bryan and I left on amicable terms and I took no animosity from it whatsoever.

As it happened Bryan only lasted a season at Bramall Lane and it ended with his expensive squad failing to make an impact on the promotion places.

After this performance against Inter Milan I was named in the next England squad.

First Premier League home kit was one of my favourite Villa kits - and haircuts!

Premier League away day action.

I enjoyed a successful spell under Big Ron.

I loved playing against Man City. A lucky team for me on the goal scoring front.

In 1994, a strong team bond was a huge factor in beating Man Utd in the League Cup Final.

Celebrating with Dalian Atkinson after one of the most exciting games of my career; the semi-final win v Tranmere.

Not stopping me today Incey - I'm on a mission!

Celebrating with Dalian Atkinson and Dean Saunders as the latter scores the 3rd and decisive goal in the Cup Final.

Against all the odds! Celebrating winning the League Cup v Man Utd in 1994. The celebrations carried on way into the early hours.

What a day! Celebrating with Andy Townsend after beating Man Utd in the Coca Cola League Cup Final.

A bit of downtime in Moscow with Carlton Palmer - posing in Russian hats, prior to an international friendly against CIS.

This is the game that booked my place in the England squad
for the 1992 Euro Finals - a 2-2 draw v C.I.S., 29 April 1992.

One of the highlights of my career,
playing for England against
Brazil at Wembley.

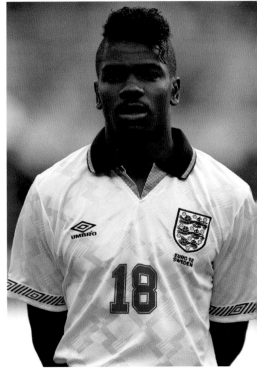

Although the 1992 Euros was disappointing
for England, it was an honour to represent
my country at a major final.

My last game for England was against Sweden in the 1992 European Championship.

A £1.25 million move to Wolves was thwarted with injury.

1995/96 season was challenging, trying to rebuild my career after serious injury.

Injuries at Wolves gave plenty of time for reflection and to experiment with new haircuts.

December 1995 - Wolves v Millwall. Last season's corresponding fixture resulted in serious injury.

Scoring and celebrating with my old team mate and friend Don Goodman.

A successful season at Watford in which we gained promotion into the Premier Leagu

A 6 month stint at Walsall was my last professional club before retirement.

Playing for Forest Green Rovers in the FA Trophy Cup Final which was my only appearance at Villa Park since I left in 1994.

Life after football - back in the Premier League as Head of Sports Science.

The other side - I had 10 very good years back at Wolves.

In memory of former England, Wolves and Aston Villa manager, Graham Taylor.

A rare appearance in '08
England Legends v Germany.

Another England appearance
England v Rest of the World.

Present- Fitness
Consultant - 7D FitForLife

Within a month I'd spoken to Barry Holmes, the former Wolves physio, who tipped my off about a vacancy at Wolves for a fitness coach. It was no foregone conclusion, just because I was a former Wolves player - I had to apply for the role just like anyone else. I spoke to Terry Connor, who was working with Mick McCarthy at Wolves about the vacancy. I knew Terry through the football network, not that well, but he knew that I had some unfinished business at Molineux and I wanted to give something back to make the club successful again. Terry Connor spoke to Mick and I was called in for an interview two days later.

I would have thought Mick and Neil Warnock had a chat about me, that's a given, about the stuff that I had done at Sheffield United, so that would have helped my cause. I was indeed successful and in September 2007, I took the role, with the elaborate title of Head of Sports Science & Conditioning.

I took over from the highly-rated Kunle Odetoyinbo, who went to Reading and had previously worked under Glenn Hoddle. I found the fitness side of things at Wolves in impressive shape. He did a fantastic job. The fitness reports were very good and he took time to show me the ropes before he left, which I was very grateful for. Of course, I wanted to do things differently – every fitness coach has his own ideas, but nothing drastic because I didn't want to change a winning formula. I was very impressed at the way the club was run and I wanted to continue that and if possible, make things a bit better.

I do believe everything happens for a reason. So, almost a decade after I had left Wolves, I found myself back at Molineux as the club's new fitness coach. It was probably meant to be as I knew Mick wanted a 'football person' as his fitness coach, rather than a data-driven person. It was ironic that I'd spent four-and-half injury-hit years at Molineux, but that only sharpened my desire to stay in the game, and now here I was occupying the bench and training pitch, rather than the physio's room. I know Wolves fans didn't see the best of me as a player and must have been disappointed but there was no one more disappointed than me. I was always well treated and there were no complaints from me. It was a frustrating time, without a doubt. Wolves had massive ambitions at the time and I was 26, at the peak of my career.

However, being out injured a lot at Wolves helped to build my knowledge of the fitness side of the game. I was always interested in that side of things and I was always asking Barry Holmes, the Wolves physio at the time, in a more detailed fashion, what my injury problems were and how they could be best treated. I wanted the ins-and-outs and I probably bored him to tears with my constant questioning. I'd always been extremely fit as a lad, in terms of trying to do things right and the education and knowledge side was something I was keen on. Barry and I used to talk about what I was going to do if I had to retire from football early. Becoming a physio was an option back then, but I was more interested in the sports science side.

I found it difficult when I first joined Mick's team because he wanted me to work around his methods for the first 10 days or so, during the pre-season; it left me itching to implement my own impetus onto the training routine. I had no problem at first in working around the existing methods as I soon found that there was a lot that I needed to change. At the end of those 10 days, we spoke about the training, where it was too much or not enough and what I could introduce. Mick wanted a high-intensity style of play but I soon found out that the pre-season training was too intense and I told Mick this, that he may have to decrease the intensity of training – I was conscious that the players may burn out before the season ended. Obviously, I had to earn the trust of Mick with what I was telling him, that everything I was saying was for the best of the players.

One of my main assets is to give everything I do 100% focus with attention to detail. One of the best things that I did at Wolves was during the final three months of the first season was to introduce GPS in the player's training regime, although I had to fight to get it. In 2007, GPS was in its infancy in football – and in team sports in general. It was really expensive – you were talking tens of thousands of pounds, but the pros of it outweighed the cons. GPS technology is used to monitor the players' fatigue during and after training and matches, and to compare intensity profiles according to the player's position. It also compares competition skill levels and identifies the most intense periods of play, including when players are playing or training too hard or not hard enough. We finished 7th that season, missing out on the play-offs by goal difference.

Wolves' aim was to be a topflight club once again. The disappointment at not making the play-offs was top of the agenda in the directors, managers and heads of department meeting; promotion at all costs next season and each department was going to be given the tools to achieve it

As soon as I'd got into my role, I started to make it my own and added one or two things to the players routine, but the one thing that I really argued for was the use of GPS technology – we really needed it, even though we were in the Championship. In the Premier League, it was fast becoming the 'norm', but in the Championship and below, the use of GPS was virtually unheard of. Mick wasn't really a 'data-driven' manager and that was partly the reason why I had a struggle to get it in, alongside the vast amount of money required to invest. A full-time member of staff would also be required to make full use of its potential. However, I persuaded the club to invest in GPS technology and in fact, got the club an unbelievably good deal with StatSports, who are now the biggest supplier of GPS technology to professional football clubs around the world. I managed to negotiate a 3-year deal that would see Wolves pay significantly less than other Premier League clubs if we went up. It was a win-win situation, because it would help our players in the long term. The club now had objective measures to assist readiness to train, and indeed to do this at the correct intensities throughout the season. Ultimately this would lead to fewer injuries and a bigger squad to pick from.

As it turned out our players were fitter than ever during that season (2008 - 2009). We were promoted to the Premier League by winning the Championship with a record amount of points and goals and played in a high intensity and dynamic manner. Our forward players Chris Iwelumo and Sylvan Ebanks-Blake, Matt Jarvis and Michael Kightly were off the charts, with the highest number of sprints, high intensity running and the amount of accelerations and decelerations. We also were top of the charts for fewest amount of injuries and training match days lost due to injury. That was testament to myself for introducing GPS technology and the whole sports science and medical department for its faultless implementation. It gave the players and the staff a new focus.

On a personal level, it was a very busy but productive season.

That same year I also completed my master's degree in applied Sports and Exercise Science. The knowledge that I gained really helped me to move the Sports Science Department forward and help improve the fitness levels of the players at the club.

Following our promotion to the Premier League, the squad were to spend 17 days in Perth, Australia for our pre-season preparations. This was a massive gamble back then because the distance and time differences meant that it could be a detrimental factor in the players' preparations. As a result, before the end of the season both Steve Kemp, who was then Head of Medical Services, and myself had to do a three-day turnaround reconnaissance to Perth, armed with a prepared list of requirements to see the training facilities for ourselves. Our mission was to see the choice of training facilities, hotels, food and amenities – it was a good job that we did. We were shown around the first hotel in Perth, a grand hotel with unbelievable facilities. They were going to close off two floors of their best bedrooms which had access to a games room and could only be accessed by the team, providing a huge meeting room that would be converted to a strength room with the requested equipment. I had a specific menu and dietary requirements that the chef would follow to the letter. There was also a swimming pool for rest and recovery. Both Steve and I were mightily impressed as it ticked all of our boxes as a base for the squad. We were going to eat in their restaurants later that evening. However, when we got to the hotel that afternoon it was quiet and subdued. When we came down for food, the hotel was unrecognisable. It was packed – I mean packed. At the back end of the hotel, unbeknown to us was a casino, which we found out was one of the biggest in Perth. To top that there was a huge bar area with at least 10 massive TV screens showing every Premier League game. Further investigation found a nightclub on the same facilities. Of course, we had to stay for a couple of hours to see just how busy it got!

That hotel, as you could probably guess, was not an option. It would be foolhardy to put players in a place with so much temptation.

The following morning, fortunately, we were taken to another hotel with similar facilities – minus the casino and nightclub. This one became our base and walking distance to our training facilities at the WACA (Western Australia Cricket Association), home of

Western Australian Cricket at that time. Originally when we had a list of three potential training facilities the WACA was second on our agenda. This trip was a classic example of the importance of doing your own reconnaissance work. The original facilities offered to us were not as seen. It was a brand-new complex, but the grass hadn't bedded yet even though they were telling us it would be by the time that we were out there in three months. In addition, there was still work to be done in the dressing room and shower areas. We were not ready to take a gamble – it had to be right. We were worried now as we thought this hotel was a banker. We travelled to the WACA with some apprehension. We shouldn't have, because the facilities were first class. As it was the cricketing off-season, the groundsman was very accommodating. The playing surface and changing facilities were immaculate. It was a win-win for me, too, as we were also able to do our conditioning runs around the field as it was equivalent to a 400m track. Given the fact it was a 5-minute jog from our base, we chose this one.

We travelled back the next day, but another part of reconnaissance was to check the effect of travel. Our club Doctor Matt Perry armed us with blue lights and melatonin supplements, plus a sleeping protocol to see if we could delay the effects of jet lag which would be very important when it came to training and playing games. We travelled business class on Emirates too, so that helped. That three-day trip was worth it, the tour was an amazing success, the squad had one of the toughest pre-seasons we put together and came back extremely fit. This definitely paid dividends as we also comfortably stayed up with two games to spare, finishing 15th.

As the seasons progressed, I became firmly part of Mick's 'inner circle' and he trusted me to give him my ideas on how we should design pre-seasons and daily training sessions throughout the season. The important thing was the results of using GPS were there for everyone to see. The team were fitter than ever and we were keeping players on the field because they were lasting the whole 90 minutes of each game. We were also experiencing fewer muscle injuries and players appeared to be training at the correct intensity. To back up all the data, we always showed the players their own stats and eventually they all bought into it because they were seeing and feeling the difference. Every Sunday evening, I'd run a report of all the data and present it to Mick and he'd study it and pick out particular stats to challenge certain individual players.

What was important to me was getting the right recovery after each training session and after each game. Post-match warm-downs have become part-and-parcel of every football club's training routine now, but back then they were hardly utilised, so that was something that I quickly introduced. Luckily, Mick's assistant, Terry Connor, was all over the information provided by the Sports Sciences department so I had his backing.

In the Championship most teams, top to bottom, had the ability to beat any team on a given day. As a result, if Wolves could improve performance by as little as two percent that could be enough in helping the team win a game, win promotion or win a cup. That one or two per-cent difference could be massive by the end of the season.

Although it took more time than I'd hoped for everyone to buy into GPS stats, it made me feel that I'd achieved something.

Even though stats were important, and became more important as time went on, the player's nutrition was also something I looked at changing. Diet is a very important part of a footballer's life so having my Sports Science degree helped me understand what the best foods are for footballers and what the best times to eat are. As a Fitness Coach, it was part of my remit to look at the diet of the players and adapt it to help with performance and recovery. It was easier to control the diet of the players at the training ground where we had our own chef than when we travelled to away games, when the team would stay in hotels and have food provided for them. It was, however, far more difficult to control what players ate away from the club.

When I first came into the role, it was a regular occurrence that the players would eat fish and chips right after a game, and if I put my sports science hat on, that shouldn't have happened – once or twice a season is not a problem, but it happened almost weekly. The previous fitness regime tried to do things right, and I'm not saying that the food was wrong, but I knew I had a lot to improve and change in order for the club to move with the times. While the players' diet allowed them to have things like protein and vegetables, pasta and rice the chef used to put a pudding on for the players, maybe once or twice a week, which in my book wasn't right. Sometimes the players would ask for a pudding and it became an almost daily occurrence. That was something I wanted to nip in the bud right away. If I remember rightly, I had a conversation with Mick about it and I explained the consequences of eating the wrong foods. I asked for more fruit to be put out around the restaurant. Breakfast as well was another time when players' diets went out of the window, with things like toast and jam, and sugar-coated cereals, so I introduced more protein-based breakfasts like eggs and more healthy cereals like porridge or whole wheat cereals. For lunches, I didn't ban pasta and rice, but it was more the sauces that I changed to healthier ones and a ban on sweet-laden puddings. Portion sizes were cut, and the way that food was cooked was changed to a healthier style – less fried foods and more baked and steaming. Fortunately, our chef, Eric was accommodating and understood the need to change. Before I came in, Eric was also accommodating with the players, maybe too much, so he had to be strict with the portion sizes and the menus. I needed to take control of what was being eaten in and around the club and he played an important part in that change.

Before anyone thinks that the players ate boiled chicken and plain pasta and lived on celery – no, that wasn't the case. We gave the players a variety of healthy, but tasty foods that looked appealing. It was a culture that I had to change, not just the food.

While I didn't make wholesale changes, I made some little changes over the course of the weeks and months. I was beginning to find my feet and trying to ascertain what I felt was right and wrong with players' diets. While the food they were eating was fine in general, I wanted to do things 'correctly' and get the players to 'the next level'. Getting footballers to that 'next level' requires the right coaching on the field, it also needs to be done off the field as well – they sit hand-in-hand. If a player is doing the right things in training, but not putting the right nutrients into their body it's not going to help the player to get to that 'next level' and they will be at a disadvantage.

I remember in my playing days, as far back as 1994 when I played for Villa, steak and chips was the 'normal' pre-match meal. While I had no problem with that, it is now a well-known fact that meat takes around 24 hours to fully digest in the body, so in hindsight, it wasn't the best thing to have three hours before a game. Even when I played for Wolves, I used to have a sandwich, chocolate bar and a bottle of Lucozade every single day for my lunch. While that doesn't seem a very healthy diet, the school of thought was that those foods could easily be burnt off during training or 90 minutes on a Saturday. That idea may still exist in some people's minds but we have moved on so far since then. We all know now that athletes shouldn't pump their bodies with anything they see just to given them energy. So much more is known about 'performance nutrition' and it's now easier to fuel bodies with the right foods in order to produce energy for their particular sport. Back then, sports science wasn't even in the vocabulary of English football clubs and even Arsène Wenger hadn't even started as Arsenal manager.

Diet is more than just food; it's also about hydration and whether players take on enough fluids before, during and after training or a match. Considering the average human body is made up of around 60% water, it's important that players get the right fluids into their bodies when it comes to preparation, performance and recovery – just a two per cent drop due to dehydration is enough to impact their game. Players' hydration status should be monitored to prevent this, plus possible heat related illnesses and fatigue

When you talk about fluids, it's now much more than just water. Footballers now have a choice of isotonic, hypotonic and hypertonic drinks. In addition, they have protein shakes and fruit smoothies. Added to that, it's important that they also have the right amount of vitamins and minerals plus supplements such as Omega 3. The one thing about nutrition is that it's very individual and you shouldn't give everyone the same things at the same times, so it was my job to tailor their 'nutrition pack' for them. That part certainly wasn't done before my arrival, so I introduced correct monitoring of food and fluid intake. Playing in the Championship every Tuesday and Saturday requires players to recover to optimal levels before, during and after games.

The job of a fitness coach in the modern-day era requires extreme dedication. I had to get up at 4:30am every day during the season to leave for the training ground an hour later, where I'd arrive at 6am. I tended to have a 45-minute gym session, shower then plan the day ahead, which included organising the players' nutrition pack two or three times a week and the players hydration levels were checked. Each player would have to give a urine sample and I'd have to check it using a portable hydration analyser (which gave results in seconds) to make sure that they were hydrated enough before training. The higher the score the more dehydrated the player was. If they were dehydrated it was my job to get them fully hydrated, by giving them the correct fluids. Sometimes, if a player was very dehydrated they were told not to train and they were given extra recovery time.

When it comes to sports science intervention, players are always looking for a way to 'beat the system.' An example of this was when players added water to the urine sample to try and lower the score and appear more hydrated and Matt Doherty was the biggest bugger for this! His hydration samples were always bordering on dehydration so he was always man marked by me to make sure that it was correct. I always remember him starting to get better results because as staff we targeted him to improve his scores which invariably would help his performance in the short term. Terry Connor was always on his case, too, to drink more fluids. After a few more weeks of well hydrated results, he suddenly started to get scores which would equate to just testing for water. He swore blind that wasn't the case, but after I got another 'monitored' sample of him before training the score indicated that he was very dehydrated. He was so confident that he had 'beaten the system' that he didn't even bother or forgot to dilute his own urine. He was subsequently fined and rightly so.

One thing I had was a good working relationship with the players. I wasn't a screamer or bawler but I understood the modern footballer and they related to that. I always displayed empathy and respect but also demanded the highest of standards. During my 10 years at Wolves, I only had to discipline a couple of players who strayed away from the required standards.

Jamie O'Hara joined Wolves for £5m after a very successful loan spell from Tottenham Hotspur. Jamie is a very outspoken individual which isn't an issue if channelled correctly. One training session when I was taking the warm up Jamie took it upon himself to say that he wasn't happy with it, "This warm up is s***! Why do we have to do this? Can't we do something different?" I asked Jamie to be quiet and to get on with it. I told him if he had an issue then when the session was over we could talk it through. However, he wasn't having any of it and he got louder and louder and things started to escalate to the point where it started to affect the whole squad. He refused to do any of the drills and urged the rest of the squad to do the same. I had no idea what his beef was because he was the only one with anything to say. Being in this game for so long you usually get a feel if players weren't happy or not having a good session. I stopped the session and told him to "p*** off into the dressing room," and whilst he was at it to explain to the gaffer why he was not going to take part in training, as he had become disruptive. Both Mick McCarthy and Terry Connor were on the other side of the field talking so initially did not pick up on the incident taking place. It was a big call by me because he had to walk past the gaffer and I could have been seriously undermined if Mick sent him back to the group because he didn't get a feel for what had occurred. The whole squad were transfixed as to what was going to happen when Mick started talking to Jamie. About one minute later Jamie trundled off into the dressing room. I knew I had taken a massive gamble as the session was a tactical one in preparation for a league game. As Terry took the first part of the session, Mick pulled me aside to say he backed my decision, but Jamie was really required for this session as he would be involved in the upcoming game. He had told Jamie to go inside and that he would be warming up with me before joining the rest of the group for the main part of the session. In addition, Jamie was to report to Mick immediately after training. That 10-minute warm-up with Jamie was silent and awkward.

The meeting following the training session saw Jamie being hauled over the coals as Mick read him the riot act, telling him that it was totally unacceptable to disrupt training sessions and to speak to any member of staff like that, and if even a sniff of it happened again, he would be fined two weeks wages. In fairness Jamie did apologise to me during the meeting. Following the meeting I pulled Jamie aside and said that if he had a problem with any session to go through the right channels and just come and speak to me afterwards. He did explain that he was going through some difficulties and had a bad day and shouldn't have taken it out on me. We shook hands and following that episode we had a mutual respect and got on very well going forward.

I was used to players moaning about training sessions, especially warm-ups or conditioning sessions. As a fitness coach you have to have thick skin because of the amount of banter and stick that you receive. I am very receptive to constructive criticism but the incident with Jamie was completely different and totally unacceptable.

It was all very intricate, but that's where my Sports Science degrees came in and played a very important part in changing the culture of training at Wolves. I must admit that it was tough, but at the same time it was enjoyable because I was making a real difference, not only to individual players, but to the team.

My day didn't end when the players went home because I stayed behind to organise and plan the next day. I had 10 years of that and I'm so grateful to Wolves for allowing me that opportunity to improve the side. The life of a fitness coach is very much a young person's game, so 10 years was enough for me.

After guiding Wolves into the Premier League in 2009 and the club maintained its Premier League status until relegation in 2011 - 2012. Mick McCarthy was sacked after a poor run of results that culminated in a 5 - 1 home defeat to local rivals West Bromwich Albion and Terry Connor took over as interim manager until the end of the season. Terry is a first-class coach with top-draw man management skills and I only have the upmost respect for him. All the players loved him and respected him. Although we initially had an uptake in our results, we struggled to avoid the drop.

Ståle Solbakken was the next Wolves manager and it was the first time that I had worked under a foreign manager. Solbakken came to Wolves with great credentials bringing in a host of new players, most of them from all over the Continent. However, he struggled to make an impact as we flitted consistently around the relegation zone and was sacked after six months.

Enter Dean Saunders.

I had played with Dean Saunders for four years at Villa – and what a player he was. However, as a manager he was totally different. He had brought in his own fitness coach, Mal Purchase, to work alongside me with the first team. I didn't have any issues with that and I was really looking forward to working alongside him if I'm honest. However, the rumour mill was in full flow that Dean originally tried to replace me, but Jez Moxey and Kev Thelwell refused this request.

What was so frustrating for me was that we would have a medical meeting to set out the physical aspects of the session for that week and Mal invariably would go and do something completely different to what was discussed. The Medical and Sports Science departments had put together specific pre-activation, rehabilitation and strength and conditioning protocols which were adhered to throughout the club to prevent injuries and to keep players at their optimum levels. As a result, there was a divide amongst the players as some no longer wanted to do specific sessions, stating that "Mal said these don't work and should do these (his)." He had a habit of going behind my back and overruling stuff which I had put in place and I wasn't happy about that. Many times, I would pull him up about this in our daily meetings and also try to talk to him privately on how we could work together to get the best out of the squad. He would listen, agree and then continue to do the opposite – it was so frustrating for me. I wasn't enjoying my role anymore and felt it was becoming untenable. I spoke to Dean about this and asked if we could have a meeting for clarity. Mal had worked with Dean at his previous clubs so quite naturally would have his ear. As a result, his answer was to crack on with it and it would sort itself out. Worst still the players picked up on this and would play one of us against the other. I'm always open to fresh ideas but Mal steamrollered his ideas through without any consultation with me – or anyone else. The rest of the staff could clearly see that I was being undermined and thankfully they had my back. We had a tight unit who supported each other; Phil Boardman, Rob Edwards, Pat Mountain, Phil Hayward, Steve Weaver and Matt Wignall were like a band of brothers to me.

During all the politics and games, we were still in a relegation battle, but I felt Dean suggested otherwise. We were eventually relegated to League One, a successive League drop, and Dean was duly sacked. About 20 minutes after the news had broken I had a phone call from Kev Thelwell (Sporting Director) to tell me that my job was safe and asked if I come into the club to discuss the Sports Science Department's plans moving forward. To be honest I wasn't bothered about the Dean Saunders sacking but gutted that we had gone from a Premier League side to League One in two seasons. Prior to Dean getting the sack, I felt that it was time for me to move on. That season had left a bitter taste in my mouth and I wanted to look at pastures new.

The very day we were relegated I wrote a resignation letter and was already going into the club to hand it to the Chief Executive, Jez Moxey. When I arrived Phil Hayward and Pat Mountain had already had their meeting with the hierarchy. I was very surprised to see Mal there, I had assumed he had been sacked as well. I went into the boardroom and before we started, handed over my resignation letter which was very PC (fresh challenge, new club and all that). However, to my amazement, they flatly refused it. I told them why I had been feeling that way and what had been going on. I asked Jez if Mal was still remaining at the club and if so, then it was impossible for me to remain there. I then explained my position, explaining the difficulties and frustration working with Mal and not being able to do my job to the best of my ability. I did not give any ultimatums as I was prepared to walk away regardless. They assured me that they were going to terminate his contract but what really made me stay was their steely determination to keep me.

It became apparent that Jez and Kev wanted a complete restructure of the whole club. Due to our successive relegations restructures would have to be made for each department. However, they recognised the importance of the Medical and Sports Science Departments and would supply a budget accordingly to get us back into the Championship. Hearing this lifted my hopes and aspirations and I began to feel that 'buzz' again. Mal left a few days later and the restructure of the club began. Incidentally, about two weeks later Dave Kelly, who was assistant manager at the time with Nottingham Forest and with whom I played alongside at Wolves (and worked with at Sheffield United), asked if I wanted to go to Forest as their Head of Sports Science. He had already spoken to their then manager, Billy Davies, and told me that the job was mine if I wanted it. If this approach had occurred prior to my meeting with Jez and Kev things may have turned out differently.

Enter Kenny Jacket.

Three weeks later, Kenny Jacket was named new Head Coach

of Wolves, tasked with the job of stopping the rot. A few days later Kenny called me into a meeting to discuss pre-season. Fitness of his players was high on his agenda. Like all managers, Kenny had a particular way that he wanted to construct pre-season. Initially I had organised the squad to have their physiological tests over a three-day period. The following week saw the squad split into groups of similar abilities for GPS monitored interval runs. Each group had specific times to complete the intervals which was dependent on their predetermined fitness levels. These conditioning runs were tough but intensity was monitored to reduce the chances of players picking up stress related injuries and to ensure players were training at the required intensity. The players would then refuel with breakfast and have a football based-session at 10am. Lunch would follow and the players would then have structured prehabilitation (prehab) and/or strength sessions at 3pm.

I had learnt quickly that you should never fight against what the manager wants during pre-season but work around it. In other words, work smartly. Kenny wanted the squad in for 7:30am for a long-distance run, then breakfast, followed by training. In the afternoon we had lunch and then a strength and conditioning session. It was music to my ears that he saw strength training and prehab as important attributes for his teams.

Kenny's structure was very similar to my protocol, the main difference was his early morning runs for the first week. I'm not a huge fan of slow, steady state running for the modern-day footballer. Way back when I was playing, yes absolutely! Players were virtually doing nothing over a six-week period and were coming back overweight and invariably unfit. The off-season represents an important time for players to fully recover, prepare for the next season and if necessary begin to rectify any physical and metabolic weaknesses that have occurred during the season. Today players are given off-season tailored programmes which include initially this type of running and thus hardly lose any base fitness.

My fear was that the impact caused by running these distances in unfamiliar footwear may cause unavoidable overload injuries at best and at worse stress fractures. I discussed this with Kenny, but he was insistent on doing them. He did, however, agree that players that we recognised as a 'red flag' should not run but still attend and complete the course by bike. This was a good compromise in my view. I understood why Kenny wanted to do these runs. Not only would players gain superior fitness levels, but it was excellent group bonding and would show him which players in the squad were resilient and had the mental capacity to cope with adversity.

However, my concern was the collateral damage. We discussed the rest of the pre-season protocol and Kenny was very accommodating and was happy with the rest of the set up. As we finished the last thing he asked me was if I was able to organise and take these runs – of course I agreed. In hindsight, this was an error on my part because I didn't take him literally.

The pre-season testing went smoothly. Day one of pre-season had been planned meticulously. For the 7:30am run, which was a forty-minute run along the canal right next to the Compton training ground, we had staff, Phil Boardman (First Team Analyst), Phil Hayward (Head of Medical Services) and myself taking the squad. Both of the Phils were excellent runners and when it came to the running they were probably as fit as the playing squad. Due to the nature of the run, I was taking part on my bike because my knee would not be able to take the strain of the terrain.

Pat Mountain (Goalkeeping Coach) took his 'keepers and a couple of players from the squad with potential injury concerns on bikes. Kenny and his assistant Joe Gallen came down to the starting area and addressed the squad, before Phil Boardman took the group from the front, me on my bike central, and Phil Hayward ran at the rear to make sure no one was lagging. There were plenty of moans from the lads once they were out of the earshot of the gaffer, even more 20 minutes in as the run became more difficult. By the end of the run and the players back at base there wasn't much moaning, just silence, which tells you that it was one hell of a run! Once the lads were cooled down and stretched off they went for breakfast. As coaching staff, we stayed out to debrief. It was strange when Kenny asked about the session as he never once addressed or even looked at me which I found strange. As we finished he asked me to come to his office. As the players were wearing GPS I assumed this was where he would want some more detail on the squad in terms of numbers. I quickly grabbed this information and headed to his office. Joe quickly left the office and closed the door behind him. In a calm manner he asked, "Why were you taking the session on a bike today?" I replied, "My knee would not have been able to take the terrain, Gaffer, so I had. . ." Before I could even explain about the fact that both Phils were superb runners, and to keep the bike also maintained the required pace, he started screaming at me, "If you're a f****** fitness coach I expect you to f****** run! When I asked you if you could take the session I didn't mean on your f****** bike!" He was raging and I mean raging. His face was crimson as he slammed his fist on the desk, threw a marker pen which he had in his hand at the time across the room. I tried to defend my corner, "gaffer, the session wasn't affected. . ." I couldn't get a word in as he continued his tirade, "I'm not f****** working with people who cannot do their job, that was an absolute shambles." This continued for what felt like another two minutes, with me either trying to defend myself or apologising for the misinterpretation from our initial first meeting, but he wasn't having a word of it. I was in a daze as his parting words to me were, "Get the f*** out of my office. I've got some serious thinking to do!"

I walked out in utter disbelief, so upset at what had occurred. Directly outside the office Alison Matthews, the club's administrator, looked at me, her eyes and mouth wide open and asked if I was OK. She could hear everything, in fact anyone that floor could too. The first team office where I was situated with most of the first team coaching staff was 10 metres adjacent to the gaffer's office. As I walked in, the staff had faces similar to Alison's. Pat Mountain closed the door behind me as I sat at my desk. Rob Edwards asked if I was OK and asked, "What the hell was all that about?" All they could hear was Kenny screaming at me. I explained what had happened and told them that I may be getting the boot. As I have said our staff were a close unit and had each other's back, many a time we have given each other the heads up or pulled each other up if we felt that something wasn't right. They said to me at no point had I done anything wrong. They were only just discussing how smoothly it went, even though, I was gutted and feared for my future under Kenny. The rest of the sessions that day were tough but I managed to get through them. That episode hit me hard! It somewhat reminded me of my early encounter with Graham Taylor – my rise as a fitness coach had been of a similar ilk to as I was a player in terms of plaudits. The managers I had worked for all believed in me and trusted my abilities for a fitness coach. I had many a rollocking as a player and fitness coach and all were because I had clearly made errors or mistakes. This, however, was different and it cut me to the core. That afternoon I took it upon myself to see Kev Thelwell, the Sporting Director, and to explain what had occurred. He told me that he had already spoken to Kenny as he heard the commotion too. Kev was great and told me that no one was getting relieved from their duties over that incident. He told me that if I continue to do the job that I have been doing so diligently over the years there wouldn't be any issues, which was so reassuring.

My main aim moving forward was to build bridges with Kenny. One of the first things I did the next day for the early morning session was to ditch the bike! I was prepared to go through the pain barrier if required to prove my worth – even if it was at the back of the group.

To be fair to Kenny he made my 'fresh start' a little easier by offering an olive branch from the very next day. There was normal communication and dialogue between us. As the pre-season and the season progressed, our working relationship did too.

As staff, during a bit of downtime in the season we would usually go for a drink locally. It was then that the incident with Kenny was brought up (Kenny wasn't there). Joe Gallen, who had worked with Kenny for many years told me that he was surprised by his reaction because although he wasn't happy about the 'Bikegate' he never gave him the impression it was to that extent. Joe indicated that Kenny had 'gone off' before to other players and/or staff at his previous clubs, but he was putting down a marker if things were not done correctly at the club

That season we walked League One and broke the 100-point barrier. I really enjoyed the three years working under Kenny and built a very good working relationship with him in the end. You knew as a player or coach where you stood with him, that's true enough. If he wasn't happy he would tell you, there were no mixed messages. Conversely, it was him who would let you know. I like that in managers. I was gutted when he was relieved from his duties.

I was pleased when ex-Villa manager Paul Lambert got the Wolves job in May 2016 following the short tenure of Walter Zenga. When CEO Jez Moxey left and the new Chinese owners FOSUN took over, I feared that Lambert would be the fifth manager out of the last six that would have lasted less than a year.

I just knew that Lambert would be my last manager at Wolves and I intended to take it all in and enjoy the season. Even though we finished a disappointing 15th, it was a pleasurable experience working under Lambert. He was very relaxed with his staff and very approachable. He was also mad keen on table tennis and most late afternoons, following training, the staff would rock up to the games room and play in an organised super competitive league tournament. I'm certain he did this for bonding purposes and to try and alleviate the tension that was inevitable at Wolves. I wasn't much of a table tennis player so would end up as umpire or just barracking the rest of the staff. These games got so ultra-competitive that Lambert actually brought his own table tennis bat in! Rob Edwards, who could play a bit too, wasn't having any of it and I remember him bringing in his brand new all-singing, all-dancing table tennis bat which, let me tell you, was NOT cheap. He would keep it safely away in his desk draw along with his three-star table tennis balls, which were kept for staff only. The players had to make do with inferior table tennis balls. It was hilarious watching Lambert play. These games were box office. He was so competitive and his mannerisms whilst playing reminded me of Nick Kyrgios; disputing decisions, trying to bully the umpire (invariably me) and cursing his opponents.

Unfortunately, Lambert fell out with the board over the world-renowned 'super-agent' Jorge Mendes' increasing influence on recruitment and was eventually relieved of his duties at the end of that season. It was Kev Thelwell who called me prior to the official announcement that I was to suffer the same fate. He was very gracious though, telling me that the board were looking at going in a different direction and it had nothing to do with my work. He thanked me for my 10-year service and said what a pleasure it was to work with me, which I reciprocated.

After a decade at Wolves my time as Head of Performance/Fitness Coach came to an end when Paul Lambert was sacked. Nuno Espírito Santo took the realm and started a new era at Molineux. In my time there I worked under seven different managers. There were plenty of highs and some lows but I really enjoyed working there. I have to say that I was very grateful for the support and belief showed in me during my tenure by CEO Jez Moxey and Sporting Director Kev Thelwell.

CHAPTER 9
The Past, the Present and the Future

"I get as much pleasure with this career as I did as a professional footballer."

AFTER LEAVING Wolves as Head of Performance in 2017, I was initially very keen to get back into football as soon as possible. Within weeks I had offers from Scunthorpe and my ex-boss Kenny Jackett at Portsmouth. I was also head hunted by West Ham. Although I was extremely grateful for the interest, whether it was the financial package or location, the roles just never seemed right. I had just received my remuneration package from Wolves as I had a one-year rollover contract and decided to take a bit of time to recharge my batteries and decide on the direction of future.

After meeting my good friend Dave Barnett for a coffee one afternoon he steered me into a new path. We both went to the same school, St. George's Comprehensive, and played in the same football teams for school and district. Although we later took different paths in our successful football careers – I went through the academy set-up whilst Dave went through the non-League route, we ended up on rival sides of the city divide as Dave played for Birmingham City.

After that meeting we decided to team-up together and set up a company called Pro-Level Performance (PLP), a football programme which saw 12 - 17-year-olds receive first class coaching, mentoring and advice. The four-step programme, which was based in Aston, and just a mile from where I grew up, saw us working with scholars on everything from a high level of technical football coaching to sports science, nutrition and mindset.

It was open to players who were either already in an academy but required an additional push, to those newly released, or those shining in the Sunday League system and needing refining for the future. Each and every player was treated as an individual. Collaborations between Pro-Level Performance, clubs and academies not only enhanced the clubs' offering, but also helped parents and youngsters too by working together holistically. As well as improving technical prowess the sessions aimed to help youngsters with cognitive support and welfare issues, as it has been found that happier players make better players. We also offered two free scholarships enabling access for all and we secured very good investment which enabled us to provide cutting edge equipment and technology.

We were doing well and expanding, providing our services externally to local schools, but in March 2020 COVID-19 hit the world and the first lockdown was implemented. Ongoing lockdowns and the inability to access our facilities or schools put an end to our dream and we had to call it a day in April 2021.

When PLP was just an idea, I had already set up a company called 7Daley Limited. I had initially set up this business whilst at Wolves as I was getting loads of requests away from football asking if I would provide personal training or fitness consultancy work. Due to the intensity of my role at Wolves, I was limited for time and only had a select few clients which I worked around my own personal time. I worked with most of my clients in their own gyms/studios. I really enjoyed that kind of work because when you work with elite athletes you are looking at marginal improvements in performance of about 2%. This may sound like a small increase but in football terms it could be the difference between success and failure. However, working with my clients I was seeing 20 – 50% differences in results.

Once I left Wolves, I utilised the fitness techniques and nutritional knowledge that I gleaned over the years working as both a football coach and sports scientist to create my own business. I developed a brand-new platform that supplied personal and online training and nutritional plans. I also launched my own range of branded supplements which are aimed at both athletes, gym users and people looking out for their wellbeing. Today, my clientele range from Premier League footballers to novices taking their first steps towards getting fit. Running your own business is very challenging I won't lie, but I get as much pleasure with this career as I did as a professional footballer.

CHAPTER 10
Playing for England

"The ultimate dream came true."

I'VE MENTIONED BEFORE that I always wanted to play for Villa and England. It is one of those things that you dream of from such a young age when you start playing football. It's not just for you but your family and friends – Mum and Dad were so proud. Dad loved his cricket. He was a big West Indies fan, and he would always want them to beat England. But to see the pride in his face when I was playing football for England was something else.

At the age of 16 when I played for the England Under-18s against Iceland, I had a particularly good game and the headline in the *Birmingham Evening Mail* suggested I was the "next Pele" or something along those lines. It was my first bit of publicity and I will never forget that, but at the time I just took it with a pinch of salt. From that day on, people started to talk about me - I wanted to be the next Mark Walters. However, that gave me the appetite to want more.

We had a strong family unit and to know what it meant to them as well, and hopefully to add some happiness to their lives, was really humbling. I wanted to do well for them just as much as I did for myself.

My England heroes growing up were Kevin Keegan, Mark Chamberlain and Steve Coppell, and I wanted to emulate them so much.

I had a successful 1989 - 1990 campaign with Villa as we finished runners-up to Liverpool and was rewarded with a call-up in March 1990 to England's B Squad for a game against

Ireland at Turners Cross, Cork. We had a very strong squad as it was the 1990 World Cup year and this England B squad, managed by Dave Sexton, were going to be considered as making a breakthrough into Bobby Robson's final 22 for Italia '90. That squad included young players like David Seaman, Tony Adams, Lee Dixon, Matt Le Tissier, David Batty, Carlton Palmer, Dalian Atkinson and Nigel Clough. However, we were comprehensively beaten by Ireland 4 - 1 after going ahead with a superb (and typical) goal from Sheffield Wednesday's Dalian Atkinson. I came on as a second-half substitute, replacing Andy Sinton. The Ireland goals were scored by a young Niall Quinn, and my future team-mate and now good friend, David Kelly.

Although I didn't make it into the Bobby Robson's 1990 World Cup squad, I was seen in the background of the video for the famous 'World in Motion' pre-tournament song recorded by New Order. However, I was riding high for Villa when Bobby Robson first picked me for England, as an unused substitute against Scotland in the game that Steve Bull came on to make his England debut back in May 1989 and scored his first international goal. While I didn't really expect to have been called up into the squad for the World Cup, not having kicked a ball in anger for Bobby Robson, I was disappointed all the same. Although my time was limited with Bobby, he was a good guy and very good tactically. To have been picked in his squad was a big achievement for me at that stage of my career and it was an honour.

Bobby was very approachable and very knowledgeable about his players. He would tell you what he thought about any game that he watched you play in and always gave you advice on how you could have improved during that performance. He was a football man through and through. Although I spoke to him quite a lot, Bobby did call me "Steve" a couple of times, which made me laugh (as in Steve Daley). Having said that, to be picked by Bobby under his remit was truly an honour.

It would be another two and half years before I would make my debut; that would be under the tenure of Graham Taylor, who, as it happened, was my England Under-20 coach back in 1987 and, ironically, he joined Villa as manager a few months later. I remember travelling as part of the Under-20's squad to Brazil. It was on that tour that I saw how meticulous and discipline-driven Graham was for the first time. I did particularly well on that tour and I could tell that he was impressed, not just with my footballing ability, but also my personality and attitude. However, I will never forget an incident right at the end of a training session near to the end of the tour.

At the end of the training all the lads used to do their own bits and pieces, with the defenders practicing headers, midfielders honing their passing range and strikers doing some finishing drills. I had just finished some crossing drills and began to walk off the field when a wayward shot by Dalian Atkinson (who was at Ipswich at the time) fell to my feet. Without thinking or indeed looking, I controlled it superbly on the full and volleyed it like a rocket in the direction of Dalian. Little did I know that Graham was walking past at that precise moment, and it caught him flush on the back of the head, some 20 metres away. It felt like everything was in slow motion as I screamed out, "HEADS!!" (a term used to alert others that an unexpected football is heading their way). Too late! Off flew his glasses, as he buckled but remained on his feet. He picked up his glasses and the glare he gave me hit me flush on the chin. As I apologised profusely, there was a deathly silence as the lads waited for Graham's response. He looked at me and very dryly said, "If your shooting was that accurate we would have won our first game more convincingly." The lads took the p*** out me the rest of the day. Thinking about it now, no wonder he never spoke to me for so long after he arrived at Villa, this must have still been in his thoughts. Seriously, I think I left a positive impression on Graham and he could see something special in me.

I had achieved the ambitions that I had growing up, to play for my boyhood club and then to play for my country and it felt amazing. Don't get me wrong, I was nervous as anything the first time I got called up. Being in the same squad as Lineker, Gazza and Barnes was very different to lining up against them playing for Villa. Training with those names at Bisham Abbey was unreal. Bisham Abbey was the old base for England (before St. George's Park was built) and it was literally a five-star hotel with first-class sporting facilities. It was only ever used by the England football squad. We had full-sized pitches with lovely surfaces, not to the standard of pitches we see in every football ground in England, but at that time the standard was high. Even though I was an established player, I was in awe of those guys. It wasn't as though I didn't know them – I had played against all of the England lads in the league, but it was completely different training and playing WITH them as opposed to playing AGAINST them – there was an added pressure on me. I had been picked to play for my country, which meant that I was one of the best English players in the country.

However, every one of the senior players made me feel most welcome. I needn't have been nervous, but I think every player gets nervous the first time they train with the England squad.

Gary Lineker was the quietest of the senior players, although he had a joke like everyone else. He was the leader of the pack, the captain-type figure that every team needs. He was organised and structured and he'd always tell you what your job was in the team.

In contrast, Gazza was a loose cannon – and I don't mean that in a horrible way.

I'd always get to Bisham Abbey early and when Gazza came in we'd have a 'normal' conversation between the two of us, but as more of the lads walked into the changing room, Gazza would start to get a bit louder and his personality would change – Gazza the Joker would appear and he'd become the Gazza we all know and love. He loved an audience but on a one-to-one, he was just Paul Gascoigne, fairly quiet and 'normal'.

Of course, I was a big fan of John Barnes and now that I was training with him I was in awe of him, I must admit he was just a normal guy who I'd chat to. He'd very often say some nice things about the way I played for Villa.

Another senior pro in the squad was Gary Pallister. I recall him saying to me, "Ah, not you again. I'm sick of playing against you – at least you're on my side this time." All that small talk with the senior pros helped me to settle into my new surroundings and took the pressure off me. It was a friendly dressing room and one that I felt at home in.

Being involved with the best bunch of footballers in England meant the training was better and more intense. I remember playing five-a-side with Gazza on my side and I'd be watching him like a spectator, watching what he was going to do with the ball next, even though I was meant to be playing on his side! I wanted to watch him do stuff – he was that good, I was in awe of him, and I was on his side – that's how good he was. I had to pinch myself.

There was a huge difference in the training and as an England player you were expected to deal with it. What I found was that you'd be given the ball in tighter areas because you were expected to control the ball better, even when you're under pressure, you were expected to pass the ball quicker in possession. When I was playing for Villa, I often found that there was more time on the ball and I'd have more time to find a pass, but with England, there was no time because there was someone there in your face.

I know it's a bit of a cliché, but to be involved with those players was a dream come true.

It was almost a year before I was selected for my debut and I can't really explain what it felt like to get on against Poland in front of a partisan crowd on 13th November 1991.

But what might sound silly is that even at a young age, it wasn't just a big ambition, I actually felt that I was going to achieve it. There was no negativity or wondering how tough it would be or if I was aiming too high – I just knew it was going to happen. I think that is sometimes the difference – and I bet the England lads would say the same now – that you develop a belief so that it's not just about saying it but doing everything you can to achieve it.

I was on the bench for 70 minutes against Poland. We went 1 – 0 down and I remember getting the first shout from Graham to go and warm-up. I think he said something like, "Go and get yourself warmed up – you'll be on in a bit." I can still feel the butterflies now, good butterflies, but at the time I was absolutely s****** myself, given the importance of the game. It wasn't a friendly and we needed a point to qualify for the European Championships in Sweden in 1992. We were 1 - 0 down and I needed to get out there and make a difference. However, when Graham gave me the nod, I had to go back into the dressing room for a wee. I was desperate; I was nervous as hell. When I came back, I did some more warm-ups and before I knew it I got called up with about 20 minutes to go. Graham told me to "do what you do." So I went onto the pitch full of hope and pride. I wanted to make the difference, not only for myself, but for the team. Those nerves disappeared as soon as I crossed that white line and all I was thinking about was to get cracking and make a difference. About 10 minutes later Gary Lineker got a typical poacher's goal for the equaliser. That was a great moment to be part of and it meant that we'd qualified for Sweden and Euro'92.

After the final whistle, I was part of the celebrations and it was a tremendous feeling just to be involved in such an important game. I felt that I was on my way to the Euros.

There was so much talk in the media (as there always is) around who could push their way into the Euro '92 squad and my name was included in that talk. I felt that I had a good chance because of two things. At that time, I was competing with John Barnes for a place in the team. He was a hard player to displace, but I was playing the best football of my career for Villa and the fact that John Barnes had done his achilles and was a doubt, laid the path for me to be included in the squad.

I was included in the pre-tournament games against CIS (former Soviet Union), Hungary and Brazil and did really well in them.

In the press before the Brazil game, the word was that I'd be starting and everyone was wondering how I'd get on against a second-string Brazil side that had players like Branco, Bebeto and Rai Souza. I was the new kid on the block but I didn't realise the expectancy put on me of playing for England – especially against a team like Brazil and at Wembley.

That day couldn't have been any better, playing for England in that iconic game against Brazil at Wembley in front of 53,000 fans. I started that game, wearing the number seven shirt, in a side that consisted of David Platt, Gary Lineker, Des Walker and Martin Keown, with Paul Merson and Stuart Pearce on the bench.

That game in May 1992, just prior to the start of Euro '92, was memorable for one incident. Gary Lineker took a penalty and tried a 'Panenka' but missed. If he'd have converted it he would have equalled Bobby Charlton's record tally of 49 goals for England.

I started on the left-wing but then switched wings frequently with Andy Sinton. Their full-backs were, Luis Carlos Winck and Branco, and both gave me a very tough game. They were extremely quick and liked to attack and get forward as much as I did. I was subbed in the 72nd minute and replaced by Paul Merson. We drew the game 1 – 1 after taking the lead through Platty with a spectacular volley and Guerriro equalised in the 61st minute. However, I really enjoyed the game and I was playing in front of my family and friends, who were watching in the stands.

Shortly after that game with Brazil, Graham Taylor named the squad for the 1992 European Championship and I had been selected. It's difficult to explain the amount of joy, achievement, humbleness and gratitude that I felt when I heard the news. I was literally on cloud nine. All that hard work and dedication to my profession had come to fruition.

Being named in the squad for Euro '92 was incredible and I always remember everything else associated with it and not just the football. I remember that you'd have companies giving away goods, such as Sega game consoles and other stuff. There were also so many media commitments to undertake, I can't imagine what it is like for the players now with everything they have to do.

However good it was off the pitch, it wasn't a great tournament on the pitch; there was a lot of negativity around the manager from the press at the time, so dealing with that was another learning process. I think everyone knows how important Graham was to me, not just to my professional career but on a personal level as well. He was always there for me and he was the same when he was England manager. Although we didn't get off to the best of starts at Villa and I regularly got 'caned' by him if he wasn't happy. If I felt I had done really well in the first half, but right at the end made a mistake by maybe not tracking back, he would go absolutely mad at me during half time. But if I came in after an absolute stinker, not being involved in anything and thinking I was going to get dragged off, he would hammer everyone else for not passing to me as I was the key for us winning the game. I would go back out feeling on cloud nine. It's the man management of knowing how to keep everyone on their toes and how to get the best out of everyone, not just me but all the players in the team.

I was one of 59 players that Graham had used during the build-up to the tournament and I was selected to start in the final group game in Solna in an effort to supply Gary Lineker with the crosses into the box. If memory serves me correctly, we had drawn the previous two games 0 - 0. I will always remember that it felt like some of the media were hoping we would lose that game which heaped a lot of pressure on the players and the manager. It was an 'Us versus Them' mentality.

I'd had no media training – it didn't exist back then anyway so we had to learn on our feet. If you had good local journalists, you'd learn from them and in the West Midlands, we had some good sports journalists such as Rob Bishop who worked for the *Birmingham Evening Mail* and the *Sports Argus* at that time, so I was lucky in that respect and I learned to trust them and learned who to speak to and who not to speak to. It wasn't that I wasn't used to the media. The local journalists were a friendly bunch and quite close-nit. All they cared about were the clubs they reported on. The local media in the West Midlands at that time were trusted by the clubs and each club had a good relationship with the local media. Very often, you'd tell someone something 'off the record' but you just couldn't do that with the national media. In fact, the local journalists always warned me to be ultra-careful and not to tell the national journalist anything that they could use for a story.

Before that Sweden game, I was asked by Graham to do the press conference with him. In that press conference I remember the media trying to get me to tell them if I was going to play they were very aggressive. They threw questions like, "Do you know if you're playing, Tony?" Of course, I either didn't know or I didn't give anything away, but they persisted, "Come on Tony, we need to know." Or something like, "Come on, we know you're playing, just tell us. Where do you see yourself playing in the team?" I was never going to give them a quote, so I shrugged off all their questions and just said things like, "I'm going to give my best for England if I start or come on from the bench." I was trying to be as diplomatic as possible, but they continued to try and smuggle a story out of me. They even tried to get me to comment on Graham's position if we lost against Sweden, to which I just said, "No comment. I'm here to play football."

It was all quite daunting and intimidating, to be put up there on a pedestal in front of the national press.

There was no positivity at all. Their agenda seemed to be to get Graham Taylor out of a job, not to win the game for the country – and it was continual. It must have got to him – that sort of pressure would have got to anyone because it was ferocious and sometimes vile. We were put in the same hotel as the press, which wasn't a very clever thing to do, so we ended up ignoring the media as we walked through the hotel. You could have cut the atmosphere with a knife. Of course, it's completely different now for the current England lads.

During that tournament we stayed in the centre of Stockholm in a very nice hotel and all our games were relatively nearby. The worst thing about staying in hotels during tournaments is the boredom when you're not training or playing. It must have been worse back then because we didn't have smart phones or iPads and the games consoles were in their infancy. There were no smart TVs with built in Amazon or Netflix apps. We did have mobile phones – just, and so we could contact our families back home. If memory serves me right, we did have a games room where we could play pool, snooker or darts. As I've mentioned previously, we did have the latest Sega handheld games consoles which were given to us.

We started that Sweden game like a house on fire. Any fears we had about losing were dispelled when Platty volleyed home Gary Lineker's cross to give us the lead after four minutes. There were a couple of chances to make it 2 - 0 but we were pretty happy to be leading at half-time. It was a complete turnaround in the second half though. Six minutes after the interval, Jan Eriksson headed home from a corner and suddenly we were on the ropes. Graham responded by sending on Alan Smith to replace Gary with 28 minutes to play. It was very much a tactical substitution and it was such a big game, but we probably didn't realise the significance. In hindsight, it was a surprise to see someone who had scored so many goals taken off. I always remember Gary as a consummate professional so I can't recall him throwing his shirt away or moaning or anything like that. In the other game in our group, Denmark went 2 - 1 up against France and we needed to hold on to have a chance of going to the semi-final, but Sweden had other ideas.

Our hopes at the 1992 European Championship were shattered by the hosts, thanks to a Tomas Brolin winner to knock us out of the tournament at the group stage. It proved to be my international swansong and a tough tournament for Graham Taylor, in particular. It is a memory that I won't forget. It's still raw. It was probably the lowest point in English football for many years. It was certainly a low point in my football life, that's for sure.

That Sweden defeat was infamous for bringing an end to the England career of Gary Lineker, substituted with the game at 1 – 1 before his retirement, one goal shy of equalling Bobby Charlton's then goal scoring record. It also signalled the end of my own international career, although mine didn't have the longevity of Lineker's.

I seem to recall Graham took a lot of flak from the media before and after that defeat by Sweden – it was utter humiliation for the man who had been a huge influence in my career. It was horrific! It seemed the media were always negative towards Graham for whatever reason. You're happy to take criticism about your performance, but when it gets personal that's too far. The way they treated Graham was a disgrace. It really hurt because we were all part of the team but he took the brunt of it. The press at that time were evil towards Graham and anyone who remembers the 'Turnip' headlines after that Sweden game will know what I mean.

The bombardment of Graham in the media seemed continual. When Graham's family were included in the media onslaught, you knew that he would be angered by this as the line had been crossed. I think I'd have been the same as well.

To make things worse, the same journalists were staying in the same hotel as us so there was no getting away from it all. We were told to ignore them if we saw them in the corridor. Of course, it's all different now; Gareth Southgate has gained the trust of the media and there seems to be a completely different attitude towards the media with the England squad.

It was a difficult tournament for everyone concerned with England but it was still one that I remember just for being involved in, although it was as good as it got as far as my England career was concerned. Following that dreadful summer, I suffered a serious cruciate injury during the pre-season with Villa that followed that defeat in 1992; it could be said tha I never had the same explosive and exhilarating speed that propelled me into the England fold under Graham Taylor. While I did manage to win the League Cup with Villa in 1994, I never got back to the England scene again.

CHAPTER 11
Racism in Football

"The challenge that people of colour have is far more daunting than that of a white person"

I'M NOT AN ANTI-RACIST activist and I don't tend to talk about it much if I'm honest, but that doesn't mean I don't care about the subject. I define a 'racist' as a non-knowledgeable person, ignorant maybe, ignorant about people. It's just that I don't bang on about the subject like some footballers do these days. I certainly don't use the subject as a political football. However, whether it's 'symbolism' or anything that brings racism to the attention of the general public it is a good thing in my book. I think too much racism is swept under the carpet and I think that's not good enough. I am certainly in the category of being 'anti-racist'. However, if anyone said to me that they were 'racist' I would be open to that if they gave me a good reason for feeling that way and I would respect their view – although I wouldn't agree with it.

While I don't really want to go down the political route in this book, I think it's easy to say 'All Lives Matter' – all lives DO matter, but at the present moment the challenge that people of colour face is far more daunting than that of a white person. It's as simple as that in my opinion. It's the view that I hold from the experiences I've had in life.

While I wasn't the first black player to play for Villa, I think (and I may be wrong) that myself and Wally were the first two to really establish themselves in the Villa team. I remember Ivor Linton breaking into the first team in the late 1970s but he only played 27 times in the five years he was at the club. I understand Villa had two Zambian players, Emment Kapengwe and Freddie Mwila, join the club around 1969 but they didn't make an impact. There may have been one or two before them too.

Around the time that I started playing in the Villa first team, in the late 1980s, I have to say that some of the fanbase were stuck in the dark ages when it comes to racism. It was around that time that racism started to rear its ugly head in society. Fortunately, I can honestly say that I was never racially abused by my own teammates throughout my football career – never. However, I was sometimes racially abused by opposing players and fans, but my way of dealing with it was to smile and showcase my God-given talents on the pitch. I think that is the way a lot of black players of that era dealt with the 'banter'. When I heard the monkey chants coming from the terraces it kind of made me want to play better. It made me a stronger person and more determined because it didn't get to me.

While I didn't really take in any racist remarks or chants from the terraces, there are two incidents that I do recall when I was a player, one at Newcastle and one at Leeds. I remember playing with Wally in a League Cup Third Round game at Elland Road in October 1985 and we were running them ragged for the majority of the game. We were winning 3 – 0 and the home fans were quiet, to say the least, until I started running down the line next to the home fans and they starting singing a racist song that I won't repeat, but it included the 'N' word. Then the other side of the ground joined in and chanted another racist song. If I remember rightly, Wally scored that day and when he went to celebrate in front of those Leeds fans they would have strung him up if they could have got onto the pitch. The hatred was intense.

I can honestly say that we experienced the worst racism that I have come across at a football ground, but it was made worse by the fact that I was a winger and close to the fans. Added to the fact that attendances back then were around 15,000 at Villa Park for example, then any chants or people shouting at you could be heard pretty clearly, unlike today, where crowds are huge and anyone shouting at you would be drowned out by the noise of the crowd. If that type of chanting happened now, the team would probably walk off the pitch and the game would have to be abandoned. The ground would be closed down and the club fined heavily.

Having two black players in the Villa team must have dissipated the racist element in the fanbase and as I said, I never had any problems with our own fans in terms of racism – maybe because we were good players and in the team on a regular basis, there seemed to be a different attitude towards 'one of our own' (or two of our own).

At Newcastle, it may have been in the same season, I got dog's abuse for no particular reason. I was only a youngster back then but I had the mental strength to cope with anything. Chanting or verbal abuse didn't usually bother me that much while I was on the pitch because I was just concentrating on the game, but those two incidents at Leeds and Newcastle seemed to stick in my memory.

I heard subsequently that our own fans were upset by the chants. I just tended to shut it all out, except for those two occasions when I heard the chants loud and clear. If anything, hearing those chants made me play even better.

Abuse never, ever put me off playing football, it just made me even more determined.

I stuck up for Ron Atkinson just after he was sacked as a pundit on ITV after he made a remark about the French defender, Marcel Desailly on air. I was quoted as saying he wasn't a racist at all, in fact how can he be? Ron was at worst, 'politically incorrect' but a racist – no!

People forget that Ron fielded (a record) three black players as far back as the late 1970s when he managed West Bromwich Albion: Cyrille Regis, Laurie Cunningham and Brendon Batson – the so-called 'Three Degrees'. All three paved the way for more black players to take up football and it silenced the racists with their incredible performances for Albion. Ron can take great credit for pioneering the emergence of black footballers in England. Ron also broke that record by fielding no fewer than SEVEN black players, including myself, in a game for Villa against Everton in October 1991. In that team were: myself, Paul McGrath, Bryan Small, Mark Blake, Dwight Yorke, Dalian Atkinson and Cyrille Regis. That game against Everton was even more symbolic; Everton were considered to be a team that didn't particularly pick black players and their fanbase was considered to be racist, but not like Leeds or Newcastle fans. Incidentally, I scored in that game and so did Cyrille.

I can only go by what I know and by having many conversations with Ron, being in his presence as a player in his team for four years and knowing him as a person in terms of how he handled me. Were things done or said that could be classed as 'politically incorrect' now, but weren't then? Yes. It's not until you think about it when you're older that you realise that some things that were said back then, Ron wouldn't get away with now. Some things were done or said, not nastily or in a racist way, but in jest more than anything. We, as black footballers in the 1980s or 1990s, didn't really think anything of those things but if the same things happened now, it would be a completely different story.

Testimonials

The author would like to thank everyone who has contributed to this section with their fabulous stories about Tony and their times with him on and off the pitch.

Mark Walters
Former Aston Villa winger 1981 – 1987.

TONY'S A GOOD few years younger than me but we first met when he was an apprentice at Villa and I'd just made it to the first team. One thing was for sure, he had his head screwed on from the very start as he studied well at school and always worked hard on and off the training pitch.

I'd always rated another young Villa player called Tony Obi, but I remember one of our coaches saying there was a better player in the ranks called Tony Daley. He then came to train with us in the first team a few times. He came across as a very keen and very humble lad and unlike some young players, he always listened to the older players. Watching Tony in training he reminded me of a Gazelle, the way he ran and his pace.

One thing about Tony, and still to this day, is he was always a quiet lad; he didn't speak a lot to the older players. Having said that, everyone spoke highly of him – nobody ever spoke a bad word about him.

Tony was always one of the best and quickest long and short distance runners in the group and was always in good physical shape. He was very dedicated and worked hard to where he wanted to get to.

I remember that I played with Tony on his debut, away to

Southampton in April 1985 and he was playing against Mark Dennis, a very physical player for the Saints. He generally had a good game and was probably man-of-the-match. In the games that I played in with him, Tony was always one of the better players, although I can't really remember any specific games. However, what stood out for me is how hard he worked in the games, that he always tracked back and did the defensive work, which was unusual for a wide player in those days. Unlike myself, who was more interested in going forward, Tony made sure he tracked back when he had to.

At that age, we didn't really hang out together as there was a bit of an age gap – I think Dales was 15 or 16 and because he never drank (and still doesn't). Even when he got into the first team fold, he didn't go out much, unlike me. He was very dedicated. Having said that, he probably went out with his mates in the area he lived in. There was the odd occasion, though, where we'd see him at the Belfry (BelAir nightclub) after the game with his mates. He'd never drink or get into any trouble, though – he was very well behaved.

There was a Christmas party that we all attended and Neale Cooper did a rap about Billy McNeill and if memory serves me right, Dales had to go up on stage (forced) to do a rap or a song, but as he was a very shy and quiet lad he didn't look too comfortable doing it. Unfortunately, I can't think of any rude stories about Dales as he was always so well behaved and never did anything controversial. Being the consummate professional, he probably left all that to the other lads. I've got nothing but good things to say about him.

I left Villa in the 1987 – 1988 season and we kept in touch. Even when I played for Rangers, I came back to see Dales. I've always had a lot of respect for him as he's a good lad and is always respectful to everyone.

Steve Froggatt
Former Aston Villa (1991 – 1994) and Wolverhampton Wanderers (1994 – 1998) winger

WHEN I FIRST met Tony at Aston Villa, I was only 14 years old, and about six years younger than him. Even at that tender age, I remember watching Tony, thinking, "that's what I want to be" because I was quick like Tony was, and I wanted to be the player he was.

Straight away, I always thought Tony took me under his wing (so to speak); neither of us knew at that time we'd be in direct competition with each other (or not as the case may be), or we didn't know that we'd move to Wolves together later in our career.

A few years later, we were put head-to-head in a weird sort of way, but I never saw him as competition for my own place in the team, simply because he was too good a mate of mine. I'm sure Tony never saw me as a threat to his position, either. It was good for the team to have two good wingers like Tony and myself, but not only that, I could play in more than one position; I could play left-back if I was asked to, but I always preferred to bomb forward.

I remember one game for Villa, one of the few games we both played in together actually, and it was against Swindon Town away in an early round of the FA Cup in 1992. It was one of the funniest games I've ever played in. I was playing left-back that day, and Tony was on the left-wing. I think we went in at half-time one up and the gaffer (Ron Atkinson) went absolutely berserk at us, but in the second-half, we destroyed Swindon, so much so that I scored the winning goal with a diving header from Tony's cross, which must have been a first. We won 2 - 1, but the highlight was that we wound up one of their players, a guy called Nicky Summerbee, all through the game. We both kept running past him and he couldn't catch us and I don't even think he knew which shirt number was running past him, either, let alone what day of the week it was. We'd say to him, "that's all you're going to see of us all day" but Nicky was one of those players who always had a nibble – he was mouthy, so we thought we'd take it in turns to sort him out that day. On that occasion, we were both just trying so hard and flying down the wings. We were sensational.

The ironic thing is that when you look at how destructive we were in the (few) games we played together, like in that Swindon game, I often wondered why we never played together very often, and especially why we never played like we did that day. For that Swindon game, Ron played me at left-back, but he often played me on the wing. I couldn't understand why he kept chopping and changing after seeing us both being so destructive in that game. Ok, we both had issues with injuries, but I also think we were 'robbed' of playing loads of games together. I found it unfair and still do.

It took me until I retired to realise how good that Villa side under Ron Atkinson really was. It was the best side that I've ever played in. That team came runners-up in the Premier League – what an astonishing side that was. It wasn't just how well we played, it was the excitement that we generated too. An example of that was the Liverpool game, or more commonly known as 'The Ronny Rosenthal game', where he hit the bar from a few yards out, right in front of the Holte End. That game was ridiculous. I don't think Tony was playing that day but I was a substitute and fell down on the touchline, laughing my head off at that miss. The atmosphere at Villa Park that day was immense.

I was a mere 'baby' in that Villa squad – a little fish in a big pond of international players, and as I was the youngest, I was the butt of everyone's joke. I was a scruffy kid with wingnuts (sticking out ears) from Lincoln, so I got hammered all the time. However, that hammering made me a far better human being. The dressing room in those days was ruthless. My only memory of my debut was nothing to do with kicking a football at West Ham on Boxing Day, it was what the lads did to my suit after the game – someone cut the arms off my new Tweed jacket and kindly made my trousers into a pair of shorts. I was devastated because we had another game on the Tuesday night and that was the only jacket and trousers that I owned as an 18-year-old YTS (Youth Training Scheme) lad. Even though I had a jacket with no arms and a pair of trousers with no legs, I put them on and walked out of the dressing room into the car park feeling like an idiot. The upshot of that was, when I came into training the next morning, there was a suit hanging up on my peg. I was so confused, looking at the new suit on the peg, I even asked Nigel Spink, who responded by saying, "Nah, it's yours, son." Apparently, the lads had a whip round to buy me a new suit.

What that taught me was, if you get hammered like I did, just take it and don't let it affect you. I took it and I soon got respected for it.

Compared to the average modern-day coach, Ron Atkinson

was never a coach in the true sense of the word – he couldn't coach himself out of a paper bag; however, what he did was truly genius; he'd mix senior players with young, flair, pacey players. He'd always tell his players to go and entertain the fans. One day, I remember coming on as a kid and Ron said to me, "Go on son, go and entertain me. If you don't beat the full-back once, do it the next time." To a footballer, that gave me the no-fear attitude to succeed. He had real belief in his players and gave us the freedom to express ourselves, and I'm sure Tony would testify to that, as he was one of those flair, pacey players himself.

When I went to Wolves with Tony in the summer of 1994, I felt that I'd earned the right to be there, after the three years in the first team at Villa. The idea of me and Tony playing on the wings was enough for me to put off signing for other teams, including some Premier League clubs. My game plan was simple. If I played a crap cross-field diagonal ball, over the top of the centre-half, I knew Tony would always run onto it and win the ball. I thought as a pair, we would be frightening; no full-backs would want to face us; we would have been a threat to any defence in that league, where the defences were slower and there would be gaps for us to exploit.

Talking about our Wolves days, I can't help but mention GT (Graham Taylor), God rest his soul. While I never played first team football for Villa under GT, he brought us to Wolves as a pair. Graham signed me at Villa as a kid, but just as I was finding my way, he left to take charge of England. Working with him at Wolves was an interesting time for both myself and Tony because we both went there with big price tags and big expectations. I say interesting, mainly because nobody spoke to either of us in the Wolves dressing room during the first couple of weeks, a dressing room that included the likes of Steve Bull, Don Goodman and David (Ned) Kelly. I guess that they thought we were two 'big-time Charlies' from the Premier League with big price tags, coming to a Second Division club like theirs.

The funny thing was, when Bully did start to talk to us, neither of us could understand a word he was saying! We'd just stand there, staring at each other thinking, "Not a clue, mate." Having said that, once we got used to his Black Country accent, Bully became a really good friend of ours.

Just like Big Ron, Graham was a one-off, but it has to be said both men were very different beasts. Graham was more like our dad because he was so disciplined in his approach to training and preparation; he hated lazy footballers and most of all, he hated lazy and scruffy footballers. I remember one time he ordered one player off the team bus because he was wearing scruffy jeans and told him, in no uncertain terms, to go home, get changed and come back when he was properly dressed. As for Ron, he was more interested in what you did on the pitch than how you looked off it.

Graham was such a nice man, a genuinely good bloke, but if you got to him he could show the full wrath of his temper and I (and I assume Tony, too) got both barrels from Graham on several occasions. It would be something like, "If you don't buck your ideas up, you can find yourself another club." It was just his way of getting into you; it was his psychology and it made you think twice about being lazy and made you train harder.

Another thing Graham hated was smug footballers. There were many times at Wolves I'd come into the dressing room after thinking I'd played a blinder, and Graham would bring me down to earth with something like, "And you, you were f****** useless. How many crosses did you get in today, son?" I sat down and wondered what he was on about – I was the best player on the pitch by a mile and here's the gaffer giving me a rollocking in front of the entire dressing room. I had no idea what I'd done wrong, but I listened to him and took it, nonetheless. One day, I told myself I wasn't having it and decided to have a nibble back – something I didn't do again. I'm sure Tony experienced something like that as well. Conversely, when he saw you needed picking up he made you feel a million dollars – he was genius at doing it.

He was a very smart man indeed and his man-management skills were brilliant. When it came to something personal, Graham was as caring as anyone (which was unusual for a footballer manager), and that's why I say he was like our dad. If anyone had a personal issue, Graham would be there to give you advice and any help you needed. I'm pretty sure Graham Taylor knew more about my family than I knew myself – it was quite scary really. And he was like that with every one of his players. He wasn't being nosey – he was totally genuine with his concern.

Tony had a hard time at Wolves and only played about 21

games in the four seasons there. It must have taken a lot out of him, not only physically but mentally, too. In our first season at Molineux Tony didn't play a single League game because he was injured, and that was followed by a patella injury in the following pre-season. I must admit that I shed a little tear for Tony when I heard he'd snapped his patella; how could someone be so unlucky with injuries, I thought. Even though I had my own injury problems, I ended up playing almost 100 games for Wolves. I feel blessed to have played that amount of games, but from Tony's point of view he had the most horrific injuries you could imagine. As a footballer, you can live with the calf strains and the hamstrings, but Tony's injuries were major ones which kept him out for six or 12 months at a time, at a period when he would have been in his prime of his career.

I remember another particularly difficult time in 1995, our second season at Wolves, when I was injured and laying in a bed in Wolverhampton Hospital following an operation and I had just been told that I wouldn't play for six months, so I wasn't feeling great. If I remember rightly, only a few days later, I was listening to the radio and heard that Graham Taylor had been sacked. It came as a blow to me personally, and I found the news hard to take; it seemed so unjust. OK, we (Wolves) had started the season poorly, and Tony was drained of confidence as he had just come back from injury himself and was getting some stick from the fans. While it wasn't the news I wanted to hear, it must have been awful for Tony as well; it must have been a particularly difficult period in time, given that Graham was particularly close to Tony and had been good to him when he was going through a tough time, personally. Graham should never have got sacked; the Chairman bottled it and made the wrong decision at the time in my opinion, but that's football, I guess.

Although we played a few games together in the first pre-season and we started to become a threat, it didn't really work out as we'd planned in the end. I really think that not playing week in, week out with Tony for Wolves will always be my single most regret in my football career. The ironic thing from Tony's point of view is that his one regret in football was that he didn't play many games at Villa with another winger in Mark Walters, who was a hero of Tony's. Football is sometimes a cruel game I guess.

TONY DALEY

Steve Staunton
Former Aston Villa defender 1991 – 1998 and 2000 – 2003.

TONY WAS a very liked and likable lad and he was always quiet in the dressing room. It's funny because he had these one-liners which were always low-key and delivered in the company of one or two people in the hope that it would be passed on to the rest of the dressing room. I was lucky enough to play with him for three years at Villa. He was a great player, too, and just a great lad all round.

Obviously the 1994 Coca-Cola League Cup Final was the standout game that we played in and I don't think we would have got to the final if it wasn't for Tony, with his contribution during the campaign. On the day, for me personally, he was a great help. I'd had a double hernia operation a month before the final, when we played a 4-5-1 formation and Tony helped me no-end on the day, with his positioning and play. He was a player that when you gave him the ball, he'd carry it the length of the field – that was his great strength, running with the ball and beating people. There aren't too many players who can do that – and Tony was that unique he could do that, on the right or left-side. Manchester United had Andrei Kanchelskis that day and he was especially helpful on that right-hand-side; he was a great form of protection as well as an outlet to give the ball to him. He was unlucky not to score towards the end of the game, to be fair to him but luckily we got a penalty when Kanchelskis handled on the line.

I was quite surprised that League Cup medal was his only one, especially considering his ability, but that's football I guess. I would imagine his injuries hampered his career a lot, which was unfortunate, and at the time we had Steven Froggatt and Dwight Yorke coming through. Like at all clubs, we had competition for places but he did well to recover and get back into the side on more than one occasion. We all know what happens in football, some managers have their train of thought and stick to it and for Tony, he had to move on in the end. What surprised me was that there weren't more clubs after him.

Now, Tony's dress sense was something to behold. I think the older he got, the younger style of clothing he wore. He must have jumped off wardrobes to be able to get into some of the clothes he wore, that's for sure.

Away from football, Tony tended to keep himself to himself. When we went out, we'd often go as a group and one particular time we went to Mauritius for a post-season game against Everton. The club allowed partners to come on that occasion, although a lot of the single lads didn't bring their girlfriends, so they went out there for a jolly boy's end of season trip and were put in a separate part of the hotel to everyone else. Tony and his then wife (Michelle) were with us in the main part of the hotel. One night, Tony, who says he never drinks, got absolutely hammered, and I mean hammered. Nobody had ever seen him drink alcohol before, but on this occasion he was legless. We kept warning him all night but he kept downing the cocktails. It was so funny, because we were watching him drink these cocktails. We actually found out later on that he'd finished off the mini-bar in his room before he came down to join the rest of the lads. He was hilarious. In the end, God love him, we had to help him back to his room. I think he must have thought it was one of those 18 – 30 holidays or something!

The next morning, of course he was hungover like crazy and he didn't even remember anything about that night. It was the only time I'd ever seen him drink, let alone legless.

David Norton
Former Aston Villa midfielder 1983 – 1988.

THE ONE THING I remember about "Dales' was that he would always take on board all the banter given to him in the dressing room by the lads; it would probably go in one ear, and out of the other, and that's the way to deal with it. It wasn't that he wasn't bothered about it, it was the fact that Tony was a happy-go-lucky kind of a guy and he could take it or leave it. That was one of the traits that a professional footballer needs if he wants to get to the top and Tony had it in abundance. Professional footballers have to have a mentality where nothing fazes them and that is what I found with 'Dales' and I recognised that from the first time we met.

Nothing bothers Tony; I don't see any resentment, any anger, any jealousy, any ego in him – definitely no ego. I just see a man who's always been the same. The Tony Daley of 2020 is the same

Tony Daley I played with in the 1980s – he hasn't changed one bit. If anything did bother Tony, nobody in the dressing room would know about it because he never let it show. Even when he was injured, he'd do his stuff in the gym and he still had a smile on his face.

Maybe in hindsight, Tony may think that was his only issue, that he should have let his feelings show?

John Sharma
Former Commercial Advisor and friend.

DURING THE PERIOD that Tony was first starting out as a player at Villa, I had invested a lot of money in Aston Villa, in terms of spending money on hospitality boxes. I was a mad Villa fan as well as a businessman.

I first met Tony through the then Aston Villa Commercial Manager, Abdul Rashid. We then spoke after a game at Villa Park in 1990 at his home in Four Oaks and we discussed a variety of things and what I could do for him as his commercial representative. From that day on, our friendship became stronger in many different ways.

I saw something in Tony as a player that was different to other players, and I thought I could represent him well, as I did a few other of the Villa players at the time. I wouldn't have called myself a football agent as such, but I represented footballers in a financial sense from an early stage of their careers.

Tony and I had some good banter. Very often I'd comment on his footballing skills, not that I was that good myself, things like, "you accidently crossed it" or "you accidently kicked it into the Holte End." I remember a goal that Tony scored against Luton, where he was "slipping all over the place and he couldn't believe the balance he had, given the heavy session he had the previous night." (Obviously he hadn't been drinking, it was my sense of humour).

There was a time when I went to watch Tony play for England against Brazil. I went to pick up Michelle, Tony's ex-wife, to take her down to Wembley. Although I knew Michelle at the time, we had never had an open chat together, but that day, we chatted away about lots of things all the way to Wembley. Michelle was so excited to be going to Wembley to watch Tony play and, although the mobile technology was very limited in those days, both Michelle and Tony did have one and managed to speak to each other in the car, while Tony was already at Wembley, preparing for the game.

We arrived at Wembley and found our seats, prime seats as well, and I could tell that she was very proud of him, representing his country in that game, especially when everyone sang the national anthem. I think hairs stick up when the national anthem blasts out at a sporting event and that night was no different. Tony has told me since, that as a player, he is as emotional as anyone in the stands; Tony is as patriotic as anybody I know and it's great to see that.

I think Tony swapped shirts at the end of the game with their number 6, Branco – I hope he's still got that shirt.

It was a great time to be a footballer in the 1990s. Our friendship progressed as the seasons went by and we used to go out a lot. In those days, it really wasn't that strict like it is now, but Tony wasn't one to drink a lot, if at all anyway; Tony was a good lad. In fact, I remember Tony used to sup an orange juice for the whole evening and he'd struggle to get to the bar to buy a round in – only joking, Tony! Having said that, we still had fun and games, even when we didn't have a drink inside us. Some of the Villa lads made fun of Tony and his clothes and his dance moves – I'm not sure where he learnt his dancing, but it was, well... different!

I think Tony owes a lot to Graham Taylor; he bought him to Wolves after 10 years at Villa, and paid £1.5m for him, along with Steve Froggatt. However, I seem to remember a host of Italian clubs coming in for Tony, just before Graham snapped him up. His career at Wolves lasted four years and 20-odd games. I guess it was Tony's decision to go to Wolves, instead of Italy and given his injuries, his career could have been very different, but who knows? Tony could have been a big star there.

I recall a pre-season trip to Austria, just after Tony had signed for Wolves, when he got injured, a patella injury I think, and that ended his season before it had even started. Mentally it affected him in a major way. Tony thought his career was over then, and it wasn't helped by the manager, Mark McGhee. He wasn't Tony's cup of tea. McGhee virtually left Tony to fend for himself and never communicated with him throughout his injury period, but the players were terrific.

Tony realised his career had been cut short by injury and the time came after he'd left Wolves that he knew he'd have to drop a division or two. He wanted to carry on playing, which was only natural. Tony then went to Watford, Forest Green and even went for trials in Israel, Malta and China.

Tony had a great career, despite his injuries. There's no doubt that Tony, if he was playing in the Premier League today, would be a great player, because he was lightning quick, and the game now is all about pace. Not only that, but the way Tony was also educated as a footballer, his game would adapt to the modern game, even though the day of the winger has almost vanished and attackers seem to be afraid of taking on defenders. Maybe one modern day player who is similar to Tony is Raheem Sterling.

Tony, in his heyday was quick and even now, given the state of his knees, I think Tony could give someone younger a good race over 60 yards.

Garry Thompson
Former Aston Villa forward 1986 – 1988.

I JOINED the Villa from Sheffield Wednesday, the season they got relegated (1986 - 1987) and was signed by Graham Turner, along with Martin Keown and Neale Cooper

I was a boyhood Villa fan, just like Tony, and had heard about him before I joined the club. He was a good few years younger than me, though. Having watched clips of him, he looked like a very quick kid. When he joined the first team fold and we played together I remember his career taking off, especially when Graham Taylor came in.

Everyone called Tony and David Platt, the 'Sons of Graham', because he gave them both every opportunity to excel. Platty obviously had a fantastic career and Tony's injuries hampered his career a bit, but he achieved his ambition of playing for England.

Graham Taylor loved to chat to his players, and after training one freezing cold day we were talking about certain things, usually talking to Gary Shaw and myself about our evening habits of going out for a pint. One day, Graham stopped us and said to Tony, "Have you ever played 10 games on the bounce?" Of course, Tony being injury prone hadn't and Graham challenged him to play 10 games to see if he could do it. I think Graham knew Tony from the England youth set-up so he was aware of what he could do, but he also knew Tony lacked confidence because he picked up a lot of injuries and was in and out of the side. Graham said, "If you play seven games and get injured, we start back at one." I think that gave Tony a bit of confidence.

I always thought Tony could do something with his career; he looked like a kid who was going places. Tony wasn't just quick and wiry; he was very strong as well. He could ride a tackle and had a trick in him. His crossing got better the more he trained and played in the first team. He had a goal in him too. The more I watched him, the more I thought that he could play centre-forward, or off a big centre-forward, flitting in and out.

Tony is the kind of player who could switch straight into the game as soon as he took to the pitch. Some of us took a few minutes to adjust but Tony switched straight on and focused on the 90 minutes ahead.

Shawy and I tended to look after the younger players, so we used to take Tony out occasionally, even though he didn't drink, of course. Shawy and I were the drinkers. Our diary consisted of BelAir on a Monday and Liberty's on a Wednesday, then we'd wind down for the game on a Saturday. Dales would come with us fairly regularly. On one trip to Marbella, Platty started to give us the cold shoulder for some reason. As it materialised, Graham had told Tony and Platty to "keep away from Shaw and Thompson" – I'm not sure why!

Tony was a great team-mate and a nice lad; nobody I've met has ever had a bad word to say about him. He's just a lovely kid. Even now, if I asked Tony to do something for me, he'd drop everything to help me. He hasn't got a bad bone in his body and always tries to help out. I remember when I did my own autobiography and did a book signing, I rang Tony and asked him to come along to sign some books with me and he obliged and came along. He'd help anybody.

However, Tony's dress sense and hair styles are another matter!

We were playing together when we got promoted with the Villa and I remember one game, Dales came into the dressing room with a strange new 'barnet'. After the usual jokes and sniggers, Tony then suggested that I pay his hairdresser a visit – so I did just that. The next day, I turned up to training with a Mohican. The abuse I took was horrendous – a 27-year-old centre-forward donning a Mohican! It struck me that Tony must go through that sort of abuse (banter) on a daily basis, with the different hairstyles that he had and the outrageous gear he wore. Even today, he wears the same outrageous stuff that I couldn't ever wear – it's the norm for him. I guess he could have been a model in his day as he loves to show his clothes off and he tends to get away with it. For most of us, we all think his choice of clothes are ridiculous.

As it turned out, Tony's ex-wife and my wife are cousins so we had quite a lot of engagement after we both left Villa and still to this day we are good friends and keep in touch on a fairly regular basis. We even went on holiday together when Tony was married to his ex-wife.

I think Tony was a fitness coach at Wolves and I was at Fulham at the time. I was doing some agency work there with Lee Chapman and after the game the Wolves lads were doing a warm-down. I pointed to Tony and said to Lee, "Look at that kid there, I'll give him about two minutes before he takes his top off." Now, Lee and I were in our 40s and our bodies had seen better times, but Tony took his top off as expected and we looked at his body and he embarrassed us to be perfectly honest. We were thinking, we used to have that body and he still has. It made us want to go straight back to the gym.

His body is brilliant, even at 50 plus it's brilliant. I know he now does videos and wears this tight gear just to show off to extenuate his muscles. He works out every day and lives right, eats the right things and fair play to him for that.

Terry Connor
Former Wolverhampton Wanderers First Team Assistant Manager to Mick McCarthy 2007 – 2012.

I FIRST MET Tony at Wolves when I was Assistant to Mick McCarthy in 2007, shortly after we took over from Glenn Hoddle. I'd obviously known him as Tony Daley, the footballer, and admired his ability, fitness and how he played the game. I didn't know Tony Daley the man though. It wasn't until we started to work together during that 2007 – 2008 season when he became our football / fitness coach at Wolves.

Being an ex-player himself, he was well-versed in terms of what players needed on the football side, but he applied the science to it really, really well and that was the beauty of Tony. To take the qualifications that he had and to move the club forward in a sports science type of way, but you still had that knowledge of knowing what the players needed to take part in a long, hard season. All of his advice and training methods were tapered to get the best out of the players for when they played football. He never lost sight that the players were human and that they had to be dealt with in a certain way. For me, because of that, he became an outstanding fitness coach who could also help on the football side, on the mental side, knowing how players would feel if they were facing an operation.

As Tony understood footballers, he may have got a bit more out of them; he knew what it meant to play the game and how footballers would feel throughout different parts of a game. All the sessions that he did, I really think the players were more in tune with him because he had been there and done that – he knew exactly what was required for each training session. For example, Tony was very astute in that if a player was feeling tired, he wouldn't say, "Just get on with it." He'd actually understand an element of fatigue that had built up in a player over a course of a number of games.

Tony knew exactly what his role was and fitted into our team seamlessly and dovetailed with everyone and made everyone's jobs easier because of his knowledge and the way that he was as a person. Although Tony wasn't a football coach, the players spoke to him about football and how they were feeling. He would be on the training pitch, alongside myself and our coaches and we would sometimes ask his advice and he would give us the benefit of his footballing knowledge – a kind of sounding board without being a football coach. The way that we worked as a team and how we dovetailed, I had no hesitation in speaking to Tony about what was required in terms of fitness routines. He actually educated me in terms of the work that players should be doing and invariably, the advice was very good.

Part of Tony's remit was to take a player from rehab and get them back to full fitness and he would have built up numerous relationships with players who were coming off the back of their rehabilitation following injury, and at all levels, not just the first team. Tony would spend as much time with each and every one of them to make sure they got what they needed. I know there was total respect from all the players who were injured because of the way Tony helped them get back to full fitness.

Tony and I lived near each other in the Sutton Coldfield area and as we got to know each other, we'd travel into training or on matchdays together. Our wives (Tony's ex-wife Michelle) would also socialise, so through our working relationship and how well we got on, it transcended over to our partners and we would all socialise in and around the Sutton area. Tony, being quite a nutritionist, would come up with crazy fads he'd follow, so sometimes we never knew what we were eating. As the eldest of the two of us, I would always tell Tony to stop messing about with all of his fussy eating and eat proper food. It was like, one week he'd eat protein, the next he couldn't eat protein. Crazy fads.

Although we never knew each other before Tony came to Wolves, we found out that Tony's son actually escorted my eldest daughter to the school Prom, unbeknown to either of us.

One story I have that made us all laugh was when we had to wear our suits on matchdays. Tony would invariably pick me up and we'd go to the pre-match meal. Whenever he'd get out of the car, he'd put his club jacket on and because he was so defined in terms of muscle definition, he could never turn the collar down at the back. I was forever having to put his collar down for him because it never sat right on his neck – he couldn't get his arms that far behind his head.

Dales is renowned for wearing outrageous clothes and one time we all went to Steve Kemp's stag do in Puerto Banús. We all got dressed up in jeans and tee-shirts to go out for a few beers and some food and we waited for Dales to come down from his hotel room. When he appeared he came wearing what could be best described as a gold-coloured string vest, gold Kylie Minogue-style hot pants and white basketball trainers and had his hair tied up.

He looked unbelievable! He looked a million dollars. Of course, he got ripped about what he was wearing but did he care about that? It was like water off a duck's back to him.

That summed Dales up.

I have to admit, if I had a body like his I'd probably wear the same!

Don Goodman
Former Wolverhampton Wanderers striker, 1994 – 1998.

IT SEEMED THAT every time I played against Tony he terrorised us so I knew what a great player he was. The overriding reason why I came to Wolves from Sunderland was because of Dales and Froggy and I thought that they would be good for me as a striker and could guarantee success for us at Wolves. The other reason why I left Sunderland was the better chances of me playing in the Premier League because I believed Wolves had the squad to get promoted. They had Dales on one wing, Froggy on the other, Steve Bull, David Kelly – what could possibly go wrong? I wanted to chuck myself in the mix, so he was one of several factors for me joining Wolves.

Unfortunately, Tony suffered a terrible injury very early on but worse still, I remember Tony was never properly fit after recovering from his awful knee injury. There were glimpses of him getting back to full fitness and I played in some of those games with him, and you could see the quality he had. The biggest thing he had was putting the fear into the defenders' eyes when he ran at them – they were just scared of him and didn't really know how to stop him.

It was a shame that he was injured so much during my time at Wolves, playing so few games together in those three or four years, but that didn't deflect what a brilliant player he was.

For someone who sported such outrageous hair styles and wore such extravagant clothes he wasn't one of the loudest players in the dressing room. However, to be fair to Dales, he remained true to himself in that respect – he is who he is. Tony doesn't worry about what anybody else thinks of his hair or clothes – he doesn't have to be anyone else because he is so likeable as he is. I've got to be honest; Tony took the pressure away from my own 'barnet!' It wasn't long after I joined that he decided to shave all his hair off, except for a little plait of hair at the back of his head. I thought, Wow! I don't know what that takes, courage or something, but I thought here's a man who is being himself. That epitomises Dales to be fair. His clothes as well, they took the pressure off everyone else – except for Froggy, I guess. Whereas Dales pulled off his outrageous clothes, you could dress Froggy in the most expensive suit and he'd still look like a scarecrow! Dales pulled off everything that he wore.

He tended to keep out of the 'prank wars' that went on in the dressing room which was just as well. We had a really good dressing room back then. You look at the characters in there, the likes of Geoff Thomas, Bully and Dave Kelly - well, everyone was a character really. It was in the days when there weren't any 'shrinking violets' and everyone had a voice and an opinion. Every Tuesday afternoon, after training, we'd all pile down to The Maid in Wolverhampton and we enjoyed a few drinks. We enjoyed working hard and playing hard. Dales wasn't a big drinker; he was a bit reserved in that respect but we enjoyed half a dozen nights out as a group during the course of our Wolves career together as well.

Tony was quite sensible, pleasant and mild mannered, enjoyed a laugh and the banter – he gave it and took it, and was just an all-round good egg, and continues to be so to this day. All-in-all, Tony was and still is just a great lad to know.

Mick McCarthy
Former Wolverhampton Wanderers Manager, 2007 – 2012.

I MET TONY when I appointed him as a fitness coach at Wolves in 2007. I only knew him as a player, not personally though. We originally advertised the role that Tony applied for and he obviously got the job. Quite clearly, he had a good interview and we were happy with him.

We took on Tony not only for his skills but because we liked him as a person; he was such a polite, lovely fella that it would be hard to take a dislike to him. That doesn't mean players could pull the wool over his eyes or get away with anything, Tony was very professional and tough in what he did.

I think Tony was my first ex-player fitness coach. Personally, I like fitness coaches who have played the game, and Tony fit that bill. They have a greater understanding of the game and about footballers; when players say they are tired fitness coaches who have played the game will understand their feelings, rather than a data-orientated fitness coach who hasn't played the game. Of course, I'm not disputing that they are all good at their job, but I prefer a fitness coach who has played the game – and I do think players prefer them too, if they have played the game. Tony was an ideal fella to be a fitness coach.

Tony was an extra pair of eyes alongside TC (Terry Connor) and myself on the side lines, even though he wasn't a football coach, he could input if he saw something that we didn't. Someone who has played as much as he had has got a good eye for things that are going on. Tony had an excellent relationship with the players; he knew their boundaries; he knew the language and he knew what to say and what not to say. He was amongst them most of the time so he acted as our eyes and ears and he was able to handle all of that. I got to know what I needed to know without every bit of detail.

However, Tony had shocking dress-sense. Having said that, I can talk because I feel well-dressed in a pair of jeans and a jumper! He made me and the rest of us look fairly staid in what we wore. Personally, I think he was trying to rekindle his youth with what he wore, although he wasn't old at the time – it was completely alien to mine, which doesn't mean it was bad. I remember a stag do in Puerto Banús that we all attended, where Tony came down wearing a string vest and a pair of gold pants. Having said all that, he had the body to show off his muscles – he was remarkably fit and strong.

Tony turned out to be a really vital part of the make-up of the staff at Wolves and helped us to get promoted and to stay in the Premier League for several seasons. I was very happy with what Tony did with the players and how fit they were under his remit.

Neil Warnock
Former Sheffield United manager, 1999 – 2007.

I LOVED TONY as a player because he was so direct, quick and exciting. As soon as he got the ball the crowd got up off their feet and they expected something to happen. That's how I liked my wingers to be as well.

Although I had two other candidates for the role of fitness

coach, Tony was recommended to me by someone. I met Tony first and I thought straight away that he was a lovely lad and said to my coaches he was too nice for us, but seriously I like people like that. He applied for the job of our fitness coach at Sheffield United – it was his first job after coming out of his university course. If I remember correctly he came to my house and we had a chat, then I challenged him to take a group of college kids through a training session or two to see what he could do and how he went about his work. Those lads loved it, having an ex-footballer taking their training session – he had those kids eating out of his hands. I wasn't particularly looking for someone with a sports science degree to be honest but after we spoke and having seen how good he was in those training sessions I gave him the job there and then.

I was that pleased with him that I didn't need to interview anyone else.

In a way it was a risk in taking someone so raw, but when I met him I liked him straight away and I thought he has to start somewhere, so why not here. I told Tony that he wouldn't get a better bunch of lads to start his career with. I said that he didn't need to change his approach with the pros and encouraged him to be confident and just be himself - just because he was new to the job didn't mean he should be in awe of it. There wasn't any animosity or any cliques in that dressing room – we were altogether. I could see he wanted to learn as much as the lads did. It was a good fit and a good recipe for everyone.

I like appointing people and giving them free range to do their job – they know the job more than me and Tony clearly demonstrated that he knew the role of a fitness coach. He was really clued up and once he knew they were a good group of lads he soon settled down. Of course, as with any new job, it took a few weeks to gain each other's trust and respect, but that's the way it is, but it didn't take long at all.

Tony came in and fitted into the group like a glove – it was superb. I think he was pleased that someone like me took him on for his first job because I just trusted him with doing his job – that was his department and I encouraged him to deal with it as he saw fit. I was always on hand if he had any problems and told him to come to see me – that was how I was with every department. He obviously knew what he was doing and at the time he offered something different in terms of the fitness routine that he planned for the players. The players knew very soon after Tony joined us what exactly they could and couldn't eat and drink and the lads really enjoyed it and took on board what he told them. We had a really good set of lads who wanted to listen and learn, especially to someone of Tony's stature as a former player. He still had a buzz about him, with him having been a top footballer and not long out of the game. The lads loved having him around because he always had a smile on his face and that was infectious.

Tony's a quiet lad but because he knew what he was doing and made his point clearly the players knew exactly what was expected of them. Some people talk for the sake of it and never get their point across, but Tony didn't have to say a lot because he had the respect of the players and they took on board everything that he said. He could say virtually anything because he'd been there and done it.

We had some good times during the four years that Tony was with us.

Andy Townsend
Former Aston Villa captain, 1993 – 1997.

WHEN I JOINED Villa under 'Big Ron' the dressing room was littered with vastly experienced players like Nigel Spink, Paul McGrath, Ray Houghton, Kevin Richardson, Steve Staunton, Dean Saunders and Garry Parker – there were a lot of very good players in that team. Then there were some who were a bit younger, our 'special' players, who on any given moment could make a difference. We had a young Dwight Yorke and Dalian Atkinson – and we had Tony!

Tony was amazingly quick, unbelievably fast and when the team were performing well, Tony was at his best and he was one of those players who were almost unstoppable – almost unplayable, even. Not only was he blessed with unbelievable pace, he had good, close ball control and he knew (and we knew) when he was on his game; it was a question of giving him the ball and letting him go and do what he did best.

Under 'Big Ron', Tony wasn't always a first-choice player, but he was always a great character and a lovely man, fundamentally a good man, a genuine guy who you could have a laugh and a joke with. However, he couldn't drink very well, let me tell you. Whenever we used to go out, after about half-an-hour we'd hear a giggle and knew it was 'Dales' after having a couple. Nobody likes it when you're not playing and you're out of the team, but Tony never let it affect his personality or the man that he was in the dressing room. He always had great belief in his own ability and the way he played. I liked that about guys like Tony who are proper team players. If he wasn't playing or had been subbed off, he would never have an attitude problem, he would always do his absolute best. No manager can ever say anything less about Tony.

In the dressing room, we used to take the 'Mickey' out of him but he'd always give it back in equal quantities. In that particular era, we had to make players comfortable in order for them to be able to perform and we provided that platform for Tony for him to do what he did best.

In the 1994 League Cup Final, in which Tony started, 'Big Ron' wasn't afraid to make changes, including playing young Graham Fenton alongside Kevin Richardson, with Tony playing up-front with Dalian Atkinson and Dean Saunders. Ron knew we needed a pacey front three against Manchester United as we needed to match their fire with our own. So, there were no surprises that 'Dales' started that day and he more than played his part. He was a key player in that final.

As a captain, Tony was a dream to manage as you'd only have to ask him to do something once and he'd do it; you didn't have to keep on telling him over and over again. As a player with natural pace, he didn't always see what a dream that was for the rest of us who didn't have that speed; they don't understand what a fabulous tool it is to have as a footballer. There were times when he had the ball at his feet and he tried to get past people and we had to remind him, "Tony, knock it past him and wave him goodbye" because that's what he could do. However, Tony was more than a pacey winger. Defensively, he would always help out and be responsible.

There were no surprises to me that he went into football after his playing days as a fitness coach and stayed at Wolves for a long time. He always looked after himself and physically, Tony was immaculate and liked his clothes. He always liked to dress up when we went out – we'd always see Tony coming from about half-a-mile away dressed in something outrageous. In that respect, Tony never let us down but he'd always look good in whatever he wore, to the envy of the rest of us.

I admired Tony a lot because he probably played a more significant role under Graham Taylor, prior to Ron coming in, but he never complained and just accepted it, got his head down and that's why, when it came to that cup final (1994), Ron was prepared to start him because attitude wise, you could always rely on Tony. Whatever he was feeling deep down, you could never really see it, you could only see the guy who was ready to play whenever asked.

My wife and I, and Tony and Michelle, and a few of the others, very often went out after a game into Meer Green (Sutton Coldfield) for a bit of grub or a few drinks and socially, Tony was always great company. I was saddened and surprised when I heard that Tony and Michelle had gone their separate ways, but whilst they were together they seemed very happy.

Although I've only seen Tony a few times since our Villa days, he hasn't changed; always up, always positive and never a doom and gloom merchant – and there are a lot of them in football, but thankfully, Tony was never one of them.

A message from our sponsors:
Nigel Waldron

AS AN ASTON VILLA supporter for the last 40 odd years I have witnessed many highs and lows during that time.

From winning the League in 1981 and then selling all my worldly possessions (which at 19 wasn't much) to go to Brussels in 1982, thinking that's where the European dream was going to end. Well, it didn't, so my grandad lent me the money to go to Rotterdam and the rest is history. The low of relegation five years later was very hard to take because Villa really should have kicked on to become one of the biggest clubs in Europe after 1982.

A couple of League Cups and Premier League Runners Up was very nice, but one of the worst years in the club history happened in 2015 - 2016. It took us three years to recover, but the good times are round the corner again.

One of the pleasures that I got over the 40-year timespan was seeing local youngsters come good. And we've had our fair share over the years with Gary Shaw, Mark Walters, Darius Vassell, Gabby Agbonlahor and Jack Grealish. All of those players had you on the edge of your seat and they all had something else in common – they should have won many more International Caps.

There is one name that's not on the list because he deserves a special mention – Tony "Arfur" Daley. I first heard of Tony when Graham Turner was singing the praises of him at a Sports Forum, held just after the had been appointed as manager. He was raving about this 16-year-old local lad, and to be honest, we had heard it all before and were more concerned in which direction the club was heading. However, at the time the club was going through a period of depressing mediocrity Tony stood out and then he really came to the party after (Sir) Graham Taylor took over.

It was during this period that I got to know Tony personally. I wondered how a such genuinely nice family orientated guy could make a career in a profession where racism was still an issue and wingers received next to no protection from officials. But he did and I guess there was a hidden streak of determination and aggression which those outside the club didn't see.

He has brought up two great kids and it's great to see him now doing so well off the pitch. He is a popular regular around the Hospitality Suites at Villa Park with his quirky dress sense that hasn't changed and he looks fitter than he did when he was a player. He has left me and many others of my generation with some excellent memories and provides an aspiring example for any up and coming professional footballer.

Nigel Waldron, 2022.
Power Minerals Limited
www.powerminerals.co.uk

A message from our sponsors: David Oliver

I'VE KNOWN TONY for over 10 years via a very good friend of mine, Garry Thompson, also an ex-Villa player who Tony played with. I used to organise 'Villa Legends events' along with Garry, mainly to say thank you to the people who have given me work.

One of the early events that I arranged was when I met Tony for the first time, and since then they have become bigger and bigger with about 50 - 60 people attending. The events turned into an annual event for about six years - it became like a school reunion, if you like.

Tony is a great bloke; meticulous, dedicated to everything that he does, has a great sense of humour, is very loyal and he'll do anything for you. I trained with Tony religiously three days a week for six years, going to the gym, and he taught me how to improve my lifestyle through healthy eating and living. Our friendship has grown over the years and I now class him as one of my closest friends. It has reached a stage that when Tony asked me if I would like to sponsor his autobiography I didn't hesitate to say yes.

As a life-long Villa fan, Tony was one of my football heroes and a great player. I always remember that when he was given the ball on the wing the whole stadium lit up with anticipation of what Tony was going to do with the ball. Tony was fast, skilful and he knew how to get people off their feet - I've not seen anyone like him at Villa Park since.

My business is called Alliance Commercial Finance based in Alcester, Warwickshire. We are an invoice financing broker, so we help businesses with cashflow requirements, and help companies find funding for outstanding invoices.

We have a good choice of lenders that we go to and we provide those choices to the people who come to us, so that they can make an informed decision. It's a very selective product but in short, if a company needs cash you know it, if you don't have it you probably need it.

David Oliver, 2022.
Alliance Commercial Finance
www.alliancecommercialfinance.co.uk

Stat Attack

	Appearances	Goals
Aston Villa 1984 - 1994	290	38
Wolves 1994 - 1998	27	4
Watford 1998 - 1999	14	1
Walsall 1999 - 1999	8	0
Forest Green Rovers 1999 - 2003	75	6
England 1991 - 1992	7	0
Total	**421**	**49**

Honours

Football League Division Two   Runners Up   1988

Football League Division One   Runners Up   1990

Premier League   Runners Up   1993

League Cup   Winners   1994

Football Trophy   Runners Up   2001

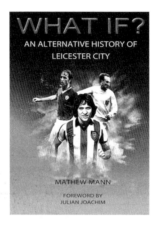
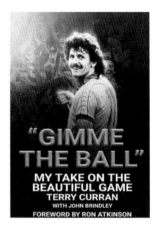

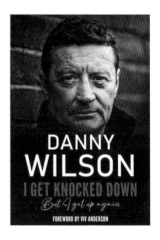